Come Alive with Kids Yoga

The 8 Steps of Yoga for Young Children

Come Alive with Kids Yoga

The 8 Steps of Yoga for Young Children

MJ "MahaJyoti" Glassman and Nancy "Niiti" Gannon

Neohumanist College of Asheville
160 Wellness Way, Marshall, NC 28753
https://nhca.gurukul.edu

Published in the United States by
Neohumanist College of Asheville
160 Wellness Way Marshall, NC 28753

Library of Congress Control Number: 2021949288

ISBN: 978-1-957460-00-0

Cover Design: Devashish Donald Acosta
Yoga Illustrations: Chitra Lani

Part One was principally authored by MJ Glassman and Part Two by Nancy Gannon

Contents

Part I: The Eight Branches of Yoga   **vii**

What is Yoga?   1
The Foundational Branches of Yoga: The Yamas and Niyamas   4
The First Branch of Yoga – The Yamas   5
The Second Branch of Yoga - The Niyamas   10
The Third Branch of Yoga: Asana   15
The Fourth Branch of Yoga: Pranayama, The Science of Breath   22
The Fifth Branch of Yoga: Pratyahara, Calming the Senses   26
The Sixth Branch of Yoga: Dharana, Concentrated Meditation   29
The Seventh Branch of Yoga: Dhyana, Sustained Meditation   33
The Eighth Branch of Yoga: Blissful Samadhi or Self-Actualization   36

Part II: Let the Fun Begin!   **39**

Yoga Drama ~ Adventure to Africa   43
Yoga Drama ~Turtle and Rabbit Race   47
Yoga Drama ~ Black Bird Gives the Best Present   51
Yoga Drama ~ Magic Cat   54
Yoga Drama ~ A New Sound   56
Yoga Drama ~ Birthday Cake Play   59
Yoga Drama ~ Mary's Little Lamb   62
Yoga Drama ~ The Butterfly's Fun   65
Yoga Drama ~ Bat's Night Friends   68
Yoga Drama ~ Rabbit's Big Sneeze   71
Yoga Drama ~ Where Has My Little Dog Gone?   74
Yoga Drama ~ Baby Crocodile Play   77
Yoga Drama ~ Jungle Play   80
Yoga Drama ~ Bear Over the Mountain Play   82
Yoga Drama ~ The Friendly Monkey   86
Yoga Drama ~ The Funny Goose   89
Yoga Drama ~ The Monster Who Stole Red   92
Yoga Drama ~ Wheels on the Bus Story   96
Yoga Drama - Paloma and its Feathers   98
Yoga Drama ~ The Costume/Halloween Party   101
Yoga Drama~ Santa Needs Help   104
Yoga Drama ~ The Lost Reindeer   106
Yoga Drama ~ The Elephant's Big Nose   108
Yoga Drama ~ Row Row Your Boat Time   111
Yoga Drama ~ Fluffy Kitten Can't Sleep   114

Part I:
The Eight Branches of Yoga

MJ "MahaJyoti" Glassman & Nancy "Niiti" Gannon

What is Yoga?

WHILE THERE ARE EIGHT major branches that define yoga, most people think of the physical postures or asanas when we speak of yoga. Yet more and more interest in the fullness of yoga is finding its way into the mainstream of yoga enthusiasts, parents, and educators who are looking for a more comprehensive and meaningful experience. The eight limbs of Astaunga Yoga include:

Yama ~ The five keys that guide spiritual aspirants in their external relationships with others and the world.

Niyama ~ The five keys that guide spiritual aspirants in understanding and balancing their internal thoughts and feelings.

Asana ~ Therapeutic body postures that are comfortably held.

Pranayama ~ Breath awareness and balance.

Pratyahara ~ Sense withdrawal from the external world.

Dharana ~ Mental focus and meditation.

Dhyana ~ Sustained concentration on the Divine.

Samadhi ~ The fullest expression of being human is realization of one's Oneness with the Cosmos.

Astaunga yoga is a systematized process for the progressive evolution of the body-mind-spirit. All astaunga yoga practices guide children towards the goal of becoming an ideal human being. These yoga experiences contribute to maximizing their potential and guiding them to the fullness of all that they can be. All activities are adapted for young children so that they are age appropriate.

Children are encouraged to consider themselves as being more than a physical body. They are spiritual beings who guard and nurture the precious Inner Radiance in themselves and in others. What is a "yoga experience" for children? Yoga is any interaction, activity, or experience that involves any of the eight branches of astaunga yoga—not just asana postures—which have been adapted to the interests of children and the general philosophy of yoga.

Children's Developmental Awareness and Yoga

Young children are entering a highly creative and intuitive phase of human development that makes it essential for yoga experiences to reflect these qualities. The young child's primary quest concerns: Who loves them? Who are they? and What can they do? The practice of yoga is where all three of these quests intersect.

Who Loves Them ~Attachment Facilitators have countless opportunities to show physical affection and caring. She can give a touch on the head or shoulder, a tap on the back, a playful wiggling of the foot as well as verbal tenderness such as "I love your snake pose." "That is an excellent choice." "I love how gentle you are with your friends." "You are such a good friend." "I love you."

The adult is always looking for ways to let children know that they are loved by the teacher, loved by peers, and, whenever appropriate, loved by the Divine. How can we refer to the Divine in a universal way and in a way that respects the diversity of the various religious paths that may be represented by the members of the group? This, of course, varies from community to community and requires some thoughtfulness. Yoga is a theistic system so it is important to find some acceptable way in which the class can refer to the Creator. Universal terms can sometimes be effective: "Inner Light," "Mother Earth," "The Force," "Mother Nature," or concepts that reflect in a universal manner something much greater than one's self.

Who They Are ~ Identity

By bringing in affirmations and framing all interactions with positivity, the teacher can support children in being all that they can be. Children can be the 'Helpers of the Universe'. They are the Light of the World. To help children embody these concepts, adults invite children to stand with their feet wide on the floor, stretching their arms high, and saying, "Shine your Heart Lights into the world. Shine happiness on the trees. Shine happiness on the animals and on your mommies. Shine your Heart Lights on _____ (name.)"

Young children are searching for their place in the world. Like the coach inspiring the sports team to be enthusiastic, to do great things, to be all that they can be ~ the facilitator brings words of inspiration, words of happiness, words for overcoming fear and self-doubt into the asana class. Children may hold a standing lunge position with arms stretched upward (Warrior 1) and repeat loudly "I am a super star! I am awesome!" Encouraging children to repeat these words loudly has the power to root these qualities in their hearts and minds, to believe and embrace their divine inner potential.

What They Can Do ~ Competence

No doubt they can hop like rabbits, slither like snakes, fly like the bats, roar like lions, and sway like the elephants. Just as the early yogis learned from and named asanas (postures) after the diversity of beings that populate the world, adults encourage physical motions with the characteristics of these animals. Be brave like the tiger. Be strong like the bear. Be graceful like the flamingo. Be fearless like the giraffe. Be swift to get away from a bad situation like the crow. Be gentle like the feather. Be sweet like the honey bee. Be beautiful like the flower. Be loud like Tyrannosaurus Rex. Be quiet like the turtle. Be helpful like the dog. Be loving like the cat.

Competency in yoga also includes enabling young children to see and understand how their actions affect others, essentially the laws of cause and effect. What happens when you use a loud voice, gently pat someone on the back, hit someone, tell someone "I like your smile," or say "Can I play with you?" Adults constantly are coaching children as to why certain behaviors and actions are preferable and why some are undesirable. They can call positive actions, "warm and fuzzy," and undesirable behavior, "cold and prickly." Empathy and kindness are constantly reinforced, being discussed at every opportunity.

Summary

Astaunga yoga empowers the all-round development of the child on every level of their being, body-mind-spirit. When yoga experiences are properly introduced, children will flourish and further their primal quests of: Who loves them? Who are they? and What they can do? Astaunga yoga practices are especially designed to maximize one's life potential in every conceivable aspect, physically, emotionally, socially, creatively, intellectually, spiritually and so forth. Within it lies the promise of a personal expansion, of a blossoming, beyond one's wildest dreams, and of offering to the limitless possibilities of engaging in the most meaningful of life experiences. It gives us the tools we need to fly.

The Foundational Branches of Yoga: The Yamas and Niyamas

Yama and Niyama encompass the ethical foundation of Astaunga Yoga. These yoga teachings delineate the dos and don'ts of our daily interactions. More than guidelines, they are the intrinsic principles that reside in the human heart. They remind us of the 'high road' that governs all relationships not only with other beings but with ourselves as well. Living by this moral roadmap children advance mentally and spiritually, living harmoniously with others. Yama and Niyama lie naturally innate and sometimes hidden or asleep in every child. Through encouragement, morality becomes important to children and enables them to form a strong mental outlook unlocking that inner door of caring and connection with all living beings and self.

Yama and Niyama are dynamic. A moment of weakness or indecision can pull a child in the wrong direction. From childhood to old age, morality necessitates continuous vigilance and introspection. Adults assist young children in rising above the ego. They acknowledge children as they are doing good deeds. "You are a good leader." "You are very patient." "I appreciate your enthusiasm." "You were very helpful." Catching children when they are demonstrating a virtue and identifying it to the child (and perhaps nearby onlookers), assists children in the ability to integrate 'higher' behaviors and understandings into their minds and hearts, to integrate these virtues in the very core of their being.

Yama and Niyama concepts are introduced at home and in class in appropriate ways through conversation, modeling, songs, discussion, stories, artistic expression, and dramatic play. By providing a clearly defined moral foundation for interaction; children's stress, frustration, and confusion are reduced. Clarity and comfort reign.

Yama and Niyama support children in properly caring for themselves and others. They enhance the internal sense of safety and comfort, as well as establishing harmony. In classes and at home, ethics create a small microcosm of what a better world can look like, enabling the young child to catch a glimpse of the Infinite in everything.

The First Branch of Yoga – The Yamas

THE YAMAS ARE ANCIENT guidelines for cooperative living. They provide guidance for navigating the turbulent waters of life with a compass of balance and compassion. The Yamas steer our relationships with human society, with the other living, inanimate beings, and the world. A clearer picture begins to emerge of how all these pieces fit together in the grand scheme of the puzzle of life. Here is a simplified version of the Yamas for young children:

- Ahimsa: Kindness, No Hurting. *I am friendly. I wear my "warm fuzzies" every day.*
- Satya: Mutual Respect. *I speak up for myself and others.*
- Asteya: Responsibility. No grabbing. *I take responsibility for my actions.*
- Brahmacharya: Unconditional Love of All. *We are different and I love you.*
- Aparigraha: Simple living. *Just two will do.*

Ahimsa or Kindness

The first principle of Yama is to do no harm. Ahimsa is to express and guide every thought, word, and action with compassion, love, and respect for the welfare of all beings. In the world of yoga this includes all that has been created, living as well as non-living entities. Yes, that includes the furniture and rocks.

Like tall grasses blowing in the wind, young children are constantly being swayed back and forth by the winds of ego. For the young child, there are three primary lessons of ahimsa: being kind to ourselves, being kind to others, and being kind to all living things. Adults stretch children beyond self-centeredness towards helping and caring for others, guiding them in the direction of expressing more sensitivity and consideration for all.

Children realize that a certain amount of conflict is a normal part of life and there are techniques for exercising self-restraint and control. Opportunities to gain self-control are given through daily activities, through stories, games, and drama to engage in problem-solving and to participate in the establishment of boundaries and consequences. Parents encourage children to think for themselves, pointing out what friends like and dislike. The benefits of self-control are addressed in discussions and daily livable moments. A perspective of understanding both sides of the conflict is encouraged, empowering children with the ability to handle conflict independently, solving their own problems in appropriate ways.

A few Ahimsa goals:

- To increase the understanding of joy and pain experienced by all people, animals, plants, and the environment due to external circumstances.
- To practice the art of initiating and maintaining friendships.
- To practice resisting the temptation of expressing disrespect or negative behavior,

particularly as retribution.
- To learn to express anger, disappointment, and frustration with benevolence.
- To develop the expression of kindness, caring for one who has been hurt.

In order to accomplish these goals, a physically and emotionally safe atmosphere is provided of mutual kindness, compassion, friendliness, and respect. Nature study of all living beings is supported to discover nature's gifts and challenges.

In a child's life many opportunities will manifest where feelings are expressed in actions and words. Adults help children to identify and understand these perhaps a little more deeply. Team building games and exercises cultivate caring and connections. Simple conflict-resolution skills are experimented with by children and caregivers. Adults may use examples of happy furniture versus sad furniture or happy friends versus sad friends.

Satya or Mutual Respect

Verbal communication is the key to expressing benevolence and mutual respect. With Satya, children learn to speak with the spirit of kindness. Differentiations between kind words and hurtful words are clearly identified. Positive supports emerge for positive benevolent choices. Of equal importance is the inner courage to stand up for what is considerate and compassionate. Gentle recommendations and coaching are required to support young children when intense feelings arise.

Children feel safe and thrive where compassionate verbal expression creates a reality filled with a high standard of integrity for all. The expression of dishonesty generally emanates from fear or an unmet need. Children's intentions are redirected towards positivity and benevolence. In such an environment they are empowered to overcome the occasionally overwhelming feelings of fear and self-doubt.

A few Satya goals are:

- To encourage better words with the spirit of sweetness in all relationships.
- To communicate intense feelings with kindness.
- To understand how to make good (but difficult) verbal choices.
- To cultivate inner strength, courage, and self-esteem to oppose hurtful thoughts and behavioral tendencies.
- To understand the effects of 'mean' language and lying.
- To stand up and speak courageously for the well-being of self and others.
- To understand the common truths of all members of the community.

An atmosphere of support and approval is displayed for children when inner courage is displayed in resisting egoistic tendencies to hurt another. Positive reinforcement like "high fives", a pat on the shoulders, privileges, and smiles are offered. Opportunities are provided to increase speaking skills with the use of appropriate tone of voice and polite consideration, giving them the words if they cannot find them. Children are supported for being truthful in the face of trying emotions. Experiences are created where they can learn how and when to speak up for self and others as well as how to say "no" with kindness.

Asteya or Responsibility

The principle of non-stealing or 'no grabbing' extends the concept of not taking possessions that belong to others to include not depriving others mentally or physically. Young children occasionally succumb to impulsive behaviors: taking objects without asking, being disrespectful of boundaries, shouting, interrupting, inattentiveness, and fighting. With tenderness, adults introduce some of these social challenges. They work with the children to create together a benevolent social system with special consideration given to the well-being of all. The responsibilities that come from living in a harmonious community are learnt.

With the emergence of understanding Asteya, children observe their relationships with objects, personal selfishness, generosity, and patience. Self-control on the physical level invariably leads to internal control as well as mental peace of mind.

A few Asteya goals are:

- To understand ownership and proper utilization of objects.
- To experience and learn how to express cooperation, generosity, and patience.
- To embrace the fairness of sharing and turn-taking.

Children in group settings understand the advantages and joys of social boundaries through continued group practice experiences. Politeness and manners are introduced. The niceties of communication are re-discovered as well as how we feel when we extend them to others. What are the benefits of turn taking? What does cooperation or moving together look like? Why can't I have my needs met right now? The knowledge of the joy of reciprocity through simple communications, of sharing, and of making others smile benefits all. New skills are practiced through role-playing exercizes.

Brahmacharya or Unconditional Love of All

To regard all objects and beings, living or inanimate, as reflections of that Supreme One embodies the very essence of this principle. We honor everyone's gifts on Mother Earth and refer to the Divine Presence in our lives according to what is culturally appropriate and acceptable. Children have a natural predisposition towards all things spiritual. However, as children grow there can occur an over-emphasis on academics and intellectuality, the acquisition of worldly knowledge. This imbalanced prioritization can leave the spiritual, the intuitive, and even creative aspects of our being far behind.

It becomes necessary to redirect the awareness toward the Inner Essence. The more children are reminded to remember the Divine Presence, the more they will be anchored to the peaceful spiritual vibration at the core of their being. This sweetness when repeatedly experienced can be easily recalled.

A few Brahmacharya goals are:

- To feel the conviction of the Inner Divine, residing within.
- To express the Divine Omnipresence in all beings.
- To maintain balance in sensory organs and personal desires.

Adults nurture the Divine within themselves and within children by introducing meditation, deep relaxation, and other experiences. Surrounding children with interactions of joy, laughter, beauty, music, and other aesthetic experiences enhances the development of internal feelings of love for the Supreme. Frequent references are made to the Divine in various ways throughout the day: We are all members of the earth family. Hurt no living thing. There is not a spot where the Divine is not.

We honor everyone's gifts on Mother Earth and refer to the Divine Presence in our lives according to what is culturally appropriate and acceptable.

Within the principle of Universal Love lies the balanced regulation of our desires, such as eating, drinking, sleeping. Adults support children in maintaining an appropriate balance in these activities.

Aparigraha or Simple Living

The balancing of attachments to sensory, physical, mental, and psychic amenities are essential to a spiritual lifestyle. Young children do not yet fully comprehend the limits and consequences of relentless desires and cravings. The practice of keeping to basic needs, comforts, and personal happiness in moderation are kept from over-flowing. An uncluttered, simple environment inviting peace and comfort will facilitate balance in a sweeter manner with smaller quantities. The spirit of moderation, love of simple living, can minimize excessive materialism, and other addictive behaviors as well as nurture the importance of pro-social behaviors.

A few Aparigraha goals are:

- To increase the awareness of materialistic simplicity and simple living.
- To understand the necessity of delaying personal gratification in deference to the happiness of others.
- To promote the understanding of how our choices impact other beings and the environment.
- To experience the joys of pro-social skills such as sharing and supporting others.

Environmental empathy is encouraged by acknowledging the various aspects of nature and their gifts. The value of recycling daily products that are used, regulating our use of environmental energy, and other resources can be made part of our daily lives. A spiritually progressive attitude calls for the respect for all, re-dedicating our lives to material and spiritual simplicity.

The Second Branch of Yoga - The Niyamas

THE NIYAMAS SUPPORT US in learning to co-habitate with all those characteristics that come together to create a human being. How to live with the ego? How to manage the mind? How to control the emotions and our desires? This is a simplified version of the Niyamas for young children:

- Shaocha: Cleanliness and Orderliness. *I put away what I use.*
- Santosha: Contentment and Acceptance. *I am happy. I can "move on".*
- Tapah: Giving and Patience. *I like to help and take care of my friends.*
- Svadyaya: Understanding. *I like to learn what my friends like.*
- Iishvara Pranidhana: Taking Shelter in Goodness. *I take shelter in "Goodness".*

Shaocha or Cleanliness and Orderliness

Physical, mental, and environmental hygiene are contingent on service to the world and humanity. Children naturally love aesthetically pleasing surroundings. However, they often struggle with maintaining neatness and orderliness. Experiences are provided for them to assist with routine cleaning and keeping the order of our environments.

Like adults, children fall victim to defective thinking and negative emotional frames of mind. These include anger, selfishness, and fear. Adults unhesitating apply various methods in a caring and respectful manner to assure that children do not linger excessively long in such negative mental states. Identifying feelings, conversing, art, nature activities, negotiation, and redirection are a few techniques that can facilitate the processing of negative emotions along with developing the skill to "move on".

A few Shaocha goals are:

- To understand the hygenic scope of physical and mental purity of self, environment, and others.
- To increase exposure of children to beautiful surroundings and aesthetics.
- To gain insights into techniques that maintain mental and emotional equanimity.

Clean and neat appearance, healthy food, and the application of strategies that instill cheerfulness and forgiveness keep us 'polished' internally and externally. While specific sanitation measures are helpful, service to others and the environment are also essential to overcoming selfishness and other forms of mental pollution. Unresolved issues can cause 'scratches' on the inner mirror of our being. These distortions or impurities need to be balanced or removed before they become embedded in the mind. The yoga practices of meditation, chanting, and kiirtan can be helpful.

Santosha or Contentment and Acceptance

The principle of Santosha is not pure bliss or happiness. It is a state of mental balance or peace that stays even when an internal struggle is still active. By nature, children are generally content with just a little if they are in a caring and supportive environment. By and large they are happy, cheerful, and carefree. Adults help them maintain a current of harmony as they expand and grow.

The state of contentment is sustained by a strong belief that there is a benevolent flow in life. An acceptance that struggles are natural and part of the learning process. Parents and teachers encourage mental equipoise and an attitude of living in harmony. We strive to not encourage either superiority or inferiority. Regardless if we are young or old, we are children of the One, Infinite Consciousness.

Excessive materialism can compromise contentment. The expansion of gratitude nurtures this delicate balance of meeting our needs without inordinate superfluousness. Santosha endures only when anchored in a universal outlook and kinship.

A few Santosha goals are:

- To maintain a balance of equanimity of mind and heart.
- To promote satisfaction in personal performance.
- To understand that unfortunate events can bring a healing balance.

To bring Santosha into full expression, life demands the cultivation of patience and the ability to shift the gears of ego, as well as intense emotion. Contentment requires being patient with oneself and being patient with others. During times of conflict, children are encouraged to see the rationale of kindness, finding joy in the accomplishments of others. A good response to a child's, "Isn't my art the best", may be "Everyone's art is wonderful, but I particularly like what you did with the yellow paint here". Self-acceptance and the cessation of making comparisons with others fosters balance.

Chanting, meditation, and other yoga practices strengthen the relationship with the Inner Divine. Nurturing Santosha requires one-pointed daily patient work in helping children to resist the charms of the ego such as inferiority and superiority complexes in their achievements, to provide experiences that encourage collective welfare, and to encourage profound trust in the wisdom of the Supreme.

Tapah or Helping Others

As young children become more mature, their capacity increases for compassion, empathy, and sympathy. Many clinical studies indicate that empathy exists in varying degrees from individual to individual. To assure its continued development, supportive activities and discussions are facilitated each day to guarantee the flourishing development of being service-minded. At the earliest age possible, children are habituated towards thinking and feeling empathy and sympathy, with an emphasis towards giving rather than taking.

Adults vigilantly watch for circumstances to engage children in helping others with minimal pressure, allowing for choices whenever possible. Tapah involves stepping a little outside of self-absorption, stretching beyond the 'me-ness', and thinking of others. Lending a helping hand to other living beings expands the mind, expands the heart, eliciting a sense of joy and meaningfulness that is self-sustaining.

Service is offered without any expectation of appreciation so that the act does not become intertwined with the expectation of reward and the development of self-pride. In this way self-esteem grows, lightening the burdens of others eventually blossoms into a naturally pleasant habit.

A few Tapah goals are:

- To sacrifice personal preference or comfort in order to help another.
- To volunteer service without expecting any personal reward.
- To make a decision, bearing in mind the well-being of another.
- To increase awareness of those less fortunate and recognize when someone is 'in trouble'.

There are many spiritual teachers today who would say that meaningfulness and success is measured not by how much money you have in your pocket but by how much you have helped others. Creating 'rescue scenarios' help children to identify people in trouble. Service activities concretely enables them to rise above selfishness and expand their inner Divine Potential. To whom is service rendered? To the Divine in the form of another created Being. At age seven years, giving without receiving anything is emphasized.

Svadyaya or Understanding

Young children are scientific explorers, making discoveries and inquiries about the mysteries of the universe with every breath. They are constantly assimilating information through all their sensory organs, formulating, reinventing a contextual framework that will serve as the cornerstone of their life experiences.

Somewhere in this landscape are the seeds from which wisdom can grow. The key to nurturing wisdom is the facilitation of interactive activities supporting the spiritual search to uncover the inner Divine. On this journey children learn to discern the nature of the many internal voices and how to realign themselves with the Inner Teacher. "I was listening to the Monster Voice when I did that." Through the blending of intuition and intellect, feeling and thinking, kids begin to grasp the building blocks of understanding to begin their pilgrimage toward Divine Wisdom, developing a relationship with the Supreme.

A few Svadyaya goals are:

- To encourage the quest to understand the root causes of the universe and self.
- To value good company and friendship while acknowledging differences.
- To have books, pictures, auditory experiences, songs, and games that reinforce the positive yoga values regarding self and benevolent interactions with others.

Implicit faith of the Supreme Presence in all living beings combined with intellectual knowledge arouses a sense of curiosity about the world. Children overcome their fear of bees, animals, and other events. Reading and re-enacting dramas with supporting breath are important tools. Doing yoga dramas with positive affirmations give children the courage to face defective thinking and build self-confidence.

Iishvara Pranidhana or Taking Shelter in Goodness

Where does the child shelter from darkness? Sheltering the thoughts in that Supreme Friend, enables young ones to move with accelerated speed towards That. In yoga, union with Cosmic Consciousness is the goal of the spiritual aspirant. This journey begins with unconditional love towards all and ends with taking spiritual shelter in the Divine (Iishvara Pranidhana). The focus is always on the Supreme Source no matter what the landscape may look like, be it bumpy or smooth.

Young children are innately connected to all things spiritual. Like magnets they are irresistibly drawn to spirituality, uplifting music, art, and the wonders of nature. They long for the spiritual re-connection with the Divine Within. To preserve this precious inclination throughout their lives, adults regularly introduce astaunga yoga practices and facilitate discussions about the Supreme. Spiritual practices include singing, dancing and chanting, yoga, listening to soothing music, relaxation, meditation, quiet time, reading and listening to inspiring stories, art, nature experiences, making music, and other uplifting encounters. These and similar activities advance spiritual attunement like a stream flowing back to the ocean, like a ray of light returning to the sun.

A few Iishvara Pranidhana goals are:

- To experience practices inspiring inner awareness and joy.
- To assist children in overcoming and re-directing fear, anxiety, and defective thinking through uplifting yoga practices. To practice yoga, stillness, relaxation, visualization, chanting, and meditation with general concepts of upliftment and spiritual progress in mind.
- To introduce devotion and unconditional love for the Supreme Entity.
- Who is your Divine Friend? Children are reminded of the omnipresence of the Cosmic Self, residing within. Emphasis is always on the unlimited infusion of positive energy and unconditional love into every dimension of our lives. All life events are orchestrated by the Supreme. Children are comforted by the diverse experiences that are offered to re-experience the inner connection of peace, joy, and unity which is the heart of all existence. May you be free from suffering. May all beings see the bright side of everything. May all beings be at peace. "Baba Nam Kevalam". Love is all there is.

The Third Branch of Yoga: Asana

THE YOUNG CHILD CAN be highly egocentric and is becoming increasingly aware of the complexities of relationships. As they begin to form relationships with the world, they tend to ascribe personal thoughts and feelings to all living beings, rocks, trees, and animals. Eager to embrace the magical aspects of life, yoga experiences are a wonderful venue for deepening their yearning to understand the mechanics of the world around them, as they explore everything, trying to make sense out of the adventure of life.

Yoga experiences for young children are expressed in the way they learn best ~ through exploration, experimentation, imitation, and creativity. Imaginative play is their bridge to reality and their methodology for learning and understanding, internalizing from experience and exploration rather than through instruction and direction.

Asanas are postures comfortably held and presented in a way that includes movement, breath awareness, sensory involvement, focus, creativity, and fun! It is important that these adventures be in alignment with developmentally age-appropriate best practices. Still discovering what their bodies can do, they thrive on investigating the world through their motor organs: jumping, hopping, spinning, crawling, rolling, flying, as well such as catching, throwing, pushing, and pulling. Arms, hands, legs, knees, and feet are engaged in active and relaxing movements. The sensory aspect is of special importance. This means showing visual pictures, making sounds, and providing kinesthetic experiences (poses that engage the hands, feet, and skin) whenever possible.

While many poses may initially resemble adult postures, they quickly morph into the world of fantasy and play, sound and movement. This is how the young brain is wired for learning, understanding, and integrating new experiences within their being.

Benefits of yoga asana

When children perform yoga, they are engaging breath awareness, new body movements and creative stretches, in rowdiness and in stillness. All children like to explore their bodies. When practicing yoga, children are discovering and observing their bodies. Yoga experiences naturally aid many physical aspects such as balance, strength, and agility, as well as enhancing proprioceptive ability or where your body is in relation to space. These postures invite them to encounter greater calmness, gain more awareness of the body, improve self-control, and self-discipline.

Yoga postures for young children are easy and not strenuous. The facilitator engages students in the culture of physical fitness, mental/emotional fitness, and the fun and caring of doing yoga with friends.

Muscles and Joints ~ Asanas improve muscle tone, strength, and balance throughout the entire muscular and skeletal systems. The postures maintain flexibility and mobility in all the joints and muscles. The weight-bearing postures, such as the cobra, plank, and balance poses aid the retention of calcium in the bones. Bone development is supported. Core strength is nourished, good posture reinforced.

Digestion ~ The challenges that may present themselves in the digestive and elimination systems can be balanced by providing organ massage in the regular practice. Digested foods are motivated to progress, triggering important acids in the stomach to be released for breaking down food and can give support to better elimination.

Respiration ~ Even though yoga asanas are performed in a slow and relaxed manner, they can improve the heart and respiratory systems. The heart rate is elevated and the cells become more efficiently oxygenated as children learn how to breathe deeper and diaphragmatically. Deeper breathing uses the space in the lungs more efficiently, decreasing negative emotional states such as stress or anxiety. The best practices for effective breathing patterns are reinforced.

Nervous System ~ There exists a rather direct relationship between the balancing of this system and breath awareness. Perhaps the most apparent benefits that clinical research have shown from asana practice are that efficient breathing reduces anxiety and other negative states of mind, inviting calmness. Emotions can be redirected. Yoga poses balance energy levels and calm the nervous system. Hyperactive and aggressive tendencies are temporarily suspended.

Twisting poses stimulate the spinal cord and nerves. Balance poses strengthen the nerves throughout the body. A sense of mental and emotional focus emerges. At the end of yoga practice, the deep relaxation pose brings all the body's systems back to a baseline level and helps children reach deeper levels of relaxation with the activation of the parasympathetic nervous system.

Mental/Emotional Balance ~ Similar to adults, children have various stressors in their lives. Events like starting school, preparing for a new sibling, moving from house to house, parents arguing, sibling fights, low self-esteem, and popularity are some of the many stressful events that affect even the very young child. Children need successful ways to manage stress and anxiety. Meditation and yoga experiences can help them to establish a more enduring mental balance.

The stillness of the poses and coordinated deep breathing effectively reduce stress and anxiety. Children learn to calm themselves with the breath exercises mentioned in the Pranayama Chapter and the simple meditations as well as chanting techniques mentioned in the chapters on Dharana and Dhyana. The regular practice of relaxing the body and deepening the breath can aid their sleep patterns.

Immune System ~ The child's immune system is supported and strengthened when reducing stress and stimulating the lymph glands. The lymph system are the body's highway of white blood cells for fighting viruses and infections. This encouragement of lymph movement in the yoga massage and asana practice is of great importance during this time when young children are challenging this system by 'catching everything that comes down the pike'. Balanced hormonal secretions within the various elements of the endocrine system is essential to fighting diseases.

Cognitive Function ~ Cognitive functions can benefit from yoga asanas. When the children do yoga breathing and postures, more oxygen circulates throughout the body and brain and can improve cognitive learning ability and memory retrieval. When children do balance poses, such as the tree or bird, children are asked to concentrate their mind on a point in front of them. This type of activity increases their attention span and the ability to focus.

Positive Social Support ~ In group yoga poses and classes, self-respect and respect of others is enhanced. Facilitators emphasize that like trees and snowflakes, no one is exactly the same but everyone is vital. The yoga poses emphasize the importance of each child's individual space and other's space. The physical and emotional boundaries are actively reinforced and nourished. Breathing in unison during the yoga session increases social intimacy and promotes an inclusive atmosphere.

As children gain more control over their bodies from their yoga practice, their confidence increases. Yoga practices gives children a positive direction to control impulses and an outlet to manage behavior. During yoga, opportunities arise for conflict resolution, turn-taking and sharing. Interactive experiences reinforce the basic yama and niyama social understandings and skills, fostering a better sense of social equity.

Neohumanism ~ At the root of yoga there is the aspect of tolerance and universal spirituality. The yoga experience invites a deeper caring relationship to the earth, humanity, and all living beings. It increases the desire to interact with others (humans and in nature) in a kind and harmonious way. A meditative awareness comes with the interest and ability to be in stillness. The understanding that we are more than our thoughts, more than our emotions, and a promise of a sense of inner contentment comes with that expression of internal and external balance. Yoga postures embody the acknowledgment of a Greater Force that is directing this amazing Dance of Creation.

Summary ~ Yoga experiences for young children strive to achieve all-round harmony of mind and body. Accommodating all body shapes and sizes, yoga is not competitive and provides exercise for the child who is less athletic. Asana practice can build a more positive body-image and greater understanding of how to maintain the health of the body/mind. It heightens the child's sensory awareness and focus.

A yoga session is resplendent with laughter, joy, and positivity. It strengthens participants' relationships and withdraws their minds from undesirable thinking. Carefully it allows the door of creativity and intuition to open wide.

How are Yoga Asanas Introduced to Young Children?

When interacting with very young children, it is important to fully understand the developmental and brain needs of each child. As you can imagine, asana experiences for the young child are substantively different than what one would see in an adult asana class. The young child loves repetition and will enjoy repeating their yoga experiences over and over. Engagement of all the senses is paramount along with increased doses of creative movement, sound, and imagination. Every pose is enlivened and energized.

Asana practice for young children is a creative, interactive experience. The asana poses do not need to be as rigid and fixed as in an adult yoga class, but more explorative and discovery-oriented. A child can be designated "Lead Child" and can interpret the pose in new ways for the other children to explore, with suggestions from the adult when needed. Classes may be a wonderful mixture of teacher direction and student direction. This fosters self-confidence, independence, and a sense of self-worth for the "Lead Child" as a valued contributing member of the community.

Tools to Help Yoga Class

Use of Yoga Cards ~ Having some sort of cards or pose representation enables the asana experience to be child-directed rather than teacher-directed. It allows the kids to make the choices and to guide the experiences rather than having the adult be the facilitator. Yoga cards can be made by the facilitator from simple photos of animals, insects, vehicles, and so forth. Calendar pictures also make excellent yoga cards. Several cards may be offered so a student can choose one to lead for the group.

Vocalization ~ Facilitators invite children to re-enact verbal sounds of animals or vehicles with yoga poses. A rhyme, poem, chant, or song may emerge. Instruments such as shakers or bells can be great additions.

Other Props ~ Scarves, paper streamers, puppets, or other representations of the animals, bugs, or items can be included in some fun way.

Words or Gestures of Endearment ~ These are offered frequently by the facilitator. The teacher will go around the room and stroke the back of each turtle or the head of each lion. Children may engage in a self-hug or hug others. Asana time is when students are complimented, by the teacher giving them words of encouragement. Teachers are constantly searching for new ways to make the asana experience more interesting. They may assist in making ocean sounds (or turning on a recording) when everyone is busy being boats. They can place a stuffed toy between the knees of each "alligator" as the alligators' mouths (the children's legs) open and shut, while everyone is chanting: "Chomp, chomp chomp."

Relationship Building ~ Opportunities to develop relationships are built into the asana experience. Seated children can pair up with feet together and hands together to sing and 'row their boats merrily down the stream.' As children move together forwards and backwards, they are reminded that "We are friendly." "We move together with gentleness." "We are being careful with our friends." Children can work as a large group seated or standing, holding hands in a large circle. They can become a great forest, a rose garden, or a giant flower that is opening and closing in harmony. New animals or insects (that may make some children anxious) may be introduced. It is presented as something positive, a wondrous creature who possesses certain gifts to the world.

Asana Methodology

At the base of asana learning is repetition. Repeating poses supports the development of determination and perseverance. Young children love repetition! The poses make physiological changes to the children. Crawling on hands and knees and crossing the front mid-line of the body engages both hemispheres of the brain. Placing the tongue on the roof of the mouth is calming. This can be done in Balance poses. Young children's bones and muscles are not fully formed so poses such as shoulder stand and other poses may not be done well but can still be adapted.

Yoga games, stories, songs, art, drama, and other expressions of creativity may also be incorporated. Creative exploration activates many centers of the brain. When introducing a pose, invite the children to find other ways to do it. Classes may be a wonderful mixture of teacher direction and student direction. Let playfulness prevail.

Make sure that the yoga experience is going to appeal to both boys and girls. Please review this list of possible asana choices: Flower, princess, butterfly, fairy, ladybug, bird, bear, elephant, hammer, helicopter, warrior, train. Will some of these appeal to one gender more than another? In order to maintain a fun atmosphere and the active participation of all children, poses must reflect their gender and individual interests.

Occupy the Mind with Positivity

Young children experience a lot of stressors in their lives and often have a difficult time measuring up to the expectations of themselves and others. They experience fear of separation, "not being good enough", and anxiety. In yoga class young children love the magical power of affirmations. These are important tools to protect their minds from negative, defective thinking. Sprinkling an occasional affirmation can support the development of their inner courage and strengthen their self-esteem.

I am kind.

I am a good friend.

I take care of my friends (family).

I am strong (brave, powerful).

I can do it!

Affirmations can be blended with powerful poses, such as warrior and hero postures. Generally constructed in the present tense, they reflect an attitude or quality that is possessed right now! They may be strongly affirmed with loud voices! As you become more familiar with the students and their life experiences, other affirmation ideas will emerge.

Asana Flow

The length of a yoga class will depend on how much time is available. It may range from ten minutes to thirty minutes. Ideally the facilitator will develop a 'certain flow' so the children can predict how the experience will unfold. Starting with a song, rhyme, or chant is a delightful way to bring everyone together. Each asana is repeated four times for maximum benefit. Having yoga cards or other representations can be helpful in guiding the class with transitions between poses.

Always a creative and experimental experience, often when children are given permission to self-express, they can become 'overly expressive' and excited. The adult will want to guide or redirect the flow from time to time. If the energy level is accelerating, what can she do to bring it down? Some background information about movement and energy can be useful. Here are some tips to assist the management of energy flow:

Back bends and movement ~ are energizing

Forward folds and resting poses (seated or supine) ~ are calming

Twists ~ are neutral

Balance poses and inversions ~ are calming

Breath awareness and meditation – are calming

If the children have performed two or three asanas such as sharks, airplanes, and gorillas, the facilitator may want to choose a calming pose like sleeping bears, rocks, snakes, and starfish-on the-ocean-floor to defuse and bring the energy level back down.

The asana class may be as simple as having a few children select some asana cards to perform. The adult may invite some interesting variations that a child may bring to a pose. One pose can morph into others such as, "Who knows what sharks eat? What would that look like? Who are some other ocean friends? (Jellyfish, seaweed, sea turtle, and others.)"

Yoga and Dramatic Play

Blending asanas with stories and other activities like games, songs, art, and drama extends as well as enhances the asana experience. The asanas become more interesting, imaginative, and accessible. Even two-year- old children find yoga poses more enjoyable when intertwined with an exciting adventure. Turning asanas into creative movement activates many centers of the children's brain. It allows children to further exert their imaginations and individualize those expressions. In this world children need not be all practicing the same poses, they can deviate and explore many creative movements. When children perform yoga to the sequences of a story, they apply their cognitive learnings and logical understandings. It is a wise investment to combine asanas with art. Many examples will follow to help adults enrich children's asana practices in Part 2 of this book.

Self-Massage

To optimize the benefits of the yoga practice, facilitators invite the children to do a neuro-lymphatic self-massage prior to the closing relaxation. Self-massage can be an important tool for a child's health. Studies show it improves the quality of general relaxation, overall resting and sleep quality, providing more energy and increasing concentration.

With the light passing of the fingers over the skin, the skin and body lymph glands are stimulated, nerve cells are relaxed, and immune function improved. A light stroking of the skin constitutes a basic foundation for the massage.

Self-massage has proven to increase dopamine and decrease cortisol levels in the body which are the "feel good" and stress hormones respectively. By reducing stress and anxiety, improved balance and well-being are assured. Massage decreases muscle tension and supports range of motion. It potentially can make children feel happier.

To introduce massage, the instructor can ask the children:

- *To give themselves a big hug.*
- *Lightly rub the bottoms of the feet, toes, ankles to knees, knees, and upper legs.*
- *Lightly massage, hands, arms to shoulders, shoulders, underarms.*

- *Touch the chest and tummies by circling the navel.*
- *Rub neck, face parts, forehead and scalp.*

Massage is followed by the traditional yoga deep relaxation posture, lying on the back with legs gently apart, arms at the sides, and head resting with eyes closed.

The Fourth Branch of Yoga:
Pranayama, The Science of Breath

YOGIS BELIEVE THAT PRANA is the life force that flows in and out of our bodies and those of all living beings. We breathe it in when we inhale and release it when we exhale. Prana is everywhere. Pranayama involves controlling the movement of energy through the use of various techniques. Every technique has a particular goal such as heating, cooling, soothing, and energizing.

Pranayama, breath control, is the heart of most practices and is what distinguishes yoga from other physical practices. Breathing is a natural and primarily involuntary process. Respiration oxygenates organs, muscles, cells, and soothes the nervous system. Pranayama incorporates controlled diaphragmatic breathing where the chest opens and the lungs expand. Abnormal breathing frequently occurs high in the chest. This can trigger the fight or flight hormonal response and can manifest as breathing at a fast, shallow pace. Shallow breathing tends to overstimulate the sympathetic nervous system and can cause other general health problems.

In Pranayama, the breath moves through the nose. Incoming oxygen is better filtered and purified with nasal breathing than through mouth breathing. Pranayama activates the relaxation response which calms the nervous system and lowers respiration and heart rate. The breath naturally becomes slower, facilitating an even deeper relaxation response.

How Is Pranayama Introduced to Young Children?

The breath rhythm has three basic parts: exhalation, inhalation, and the pauses in between. Most forms of yoga breath retention and other adult practices are not recommended for children because their nervous system and lungs are not fully developed until years later. With younger children the emphasis is on the inflowing or inhalation, and the out-flowing or exhalation. This can be further simplified by saying "breathing in" and "breathing out".

Breath patterns have a profound effect on our emotional well-being. Many young children who experience high stress begin to develop improper or reverse breath patterns. Unhealthy breathing can be imprinted on children by their parents or by new stressors. It is the teacher's aim to support young children in the following ways:

- To be able to slow down and deepen their breathing
- To enhance their awareness of the breath
- To provide abdominal breathing experiences
- To increase their understanding of how breath can be used to manage stress.

Pranayama Benefits

Medical studies have confirmed that there is a correlation between breath, thought, and many physiological responses. A harmonious mind is created and sustained by slow, deep, and regular abdominal respiration. Proper breathing is one of the keys to a balanced mental state.

Yogic breathing is closely connected to the abilities of retrieving memory and learning. We learn better when the breathing is calm. The calmer and steadier the breathing is, the stronger the power of mental receptivity. Children's learning capacity can be enhanced with a calm body and calm mind. The retentive power wanes tremendously during physical or mental restlessness and anxiety.

Oxygen purifies the blood and is good for preserving the harmony of the nervous system. Full oxygenation of the blood and organs invigorates the body, inspires the mind, and gives a sense of well-being and contentment. By learning the science of pranayama, children become aware of how a calm mind is associated with deep breathing.

Pranayama Methodology

Breathing is taking in oxygen found in the air. What is air? The existence of something invisible such as air can be demonstrated with young children in many ways:
- Blowing up balloons and allowing them to deflate around the room.
- Making paper fans and then having the children fan themselves. "Can you feel that? Can you feel the air touching your face?"
- Taking students outside on a windy day and letting them observe the effects of the wind.
- Blowing feathers or bubbles and catching them.

Reclining Belly Breathing

Children can become more aware of abdominal breathing with the following steps:
1. Children lie on their backs and place a small stuffed animal or toy on their bellies.
2. Close the mouth and breathe through your nose. Watch the toy go up and down as you breathe and pooch out your belly. Now it is going up. Now it is going down. Now it is going up. Now it is going down.
3. Use the breath to move the toy. (Continue for 1-2 minutes or until someone gets restless.)

Yoga Breath Centering for Young Children

There are various breathing games involving breath to help children slow and focus on the breathing process. To reap the benefits of these breath exercises, please repeat 3-5 times.

Ahhh Breath ~ Breathe in. Bend forward and dive down while breathing out, a long loud "ahhh" breath. Return up, breathing in. Repeat. (Can be performed seated or standing)

Balloon Breath ~ Place your hands on your belly button. When you breathe in, breathe all the way down to your hands. Feel your tummy expand like a balloon. Breathe out and the balloon gets smaller and flatter. Breathe into your balloon and watch it grow. Breathe out and let it go flat. What color is your balloon? Make your balloon belly really big. This can be practiced lying down with the hand resting on the belly (the best benefits) or with a toy on the belly or sitting with the hands on the belly, or even standing.

Bee Breath ~ While seated, pretend you are a bee. Breathe into your balloon belly. Place your hands over your ears and breathe out, making a very high-pitched "hum" like a bee. Make it loud. Make it long. Repeat. After practicing this seated, let's do this while flying around the room!

Big Bird Breath ~ Stand and breathe in. Lift your arm-wings high above your heads towards the sun. Breathe out, dive or bend forward. Touch your wingtips to the earth.

Chopping Wood Breath ~ Stand with the feet wide apart. Join your hands together as if holding an ax in front. Breathe in and raise the interlaced hands high overhead. Stop for a moment. Breathe out and swing the arms downward, holding the ax, with a loud "ha" sound. Knees may or may not bend as the ax descends. Breathing in, swing the ax high overhead and repeat once or twice again, breathing out as the ax swings down low with a "ha". (The ax can transform into a hammer if they do not understand what an ax is.)

Dragon Breath ~ Breathe in. When breathing out: ROOAARR. You may show your dragon talons.

Mother Earth Breathing ~ Breathe in. I feel happy. Breathe out. I feel happy. Pretend all of Mother Earth's children are breathing with you. Raccoon, Eagle, Rabbit, Bear, Whale, Ant, Tree. They are all breathing with you. (Seated or supine)

Rabbit Breath ~ From a kneeling position with the buttocks resting on the heels, breathe in through your nose with 3 quick breaths. (Sniff. Sniff. Sniff.) Breathe out through the nose in one long breath while folding downward, bringing your forehead to the earth. You are coming down, down into your safe home in the earth.

Shh Breath ~ From a "Criss Cross Applesauce" position, breathe in. Place your pointer finger (vertically) over your lips and breathe out a long ssshh, making eye contact moving your head, looking at each person in the room one at a time. Done in one big long breath. Can be repeated.

Snake Breath ~ While seated or in cobra pose, simply breathe in through the nose. Breathe out and make a hissing sound, slowly, slowly as you lower your snake head towards earth in the cobra pose. (Ideally, the exhalation is lo-o-o-o-nger than the inhalation.)

Sunshine Breath ~ From a standing position, breathe in as you reach up with your arms towards Father Sun. Grab some sun! Breathe out as you bring the handfuls of sun into your heart. Hold that sunshine in your heart with your hands crossed over the heart. (Add a song or chant if you like.)

Smell the Flower and Blow out the Candle ~ Curl your fingers a little on one hand so that it resembles an open flower with the palm facing up. Hold the pointer finger up on the other hand, pointing towards the sky. Smell the flower with your nose in your flower hand (curled fingers), then lean towards the other hand (pointer finger hand) and blow out the candle in your candle finger.

Pranayama Flow

Pranayama or creative breathing exercises can be practiced at the beginning of yoga class as a centering practice, or go in the middle of class, and/or at the end. Often breathing exercises lead into chanting and meditation. It is very helpful to create Breathing Cards. Breath Cards can be made with photos of the children doing a particular breath exercise or pictures of the animals or plants represented in the breath exercise.

When facilitating a breathing experience, remember that the goal is to achieve a particular uplifting and fun mental/emotional state of balance. This state of mind is the response to this physiological exercise. Consequently, all breath experiences should be repeated three to five times in order to bring this result. If a total of one to three breath cards are chosen in a class, for example, that is a total of perhaps up to fifteen breaths to recalibrate the physical body/mind in an effort to evoke the desired mental/emotional response. In addition, you will notice that all of these exercises have one thing in common. They all lengthen the exhalation breath. This is another essential physiological part of this process. Breath awareness is one of the major keys for a balanced mental and emotional state.

When facilitating simple Pranayama experiences, it is important to always surround these activities with the higher feelings of love, goodness, happiness, and that sense of being surrounded by love, caring, and positivity. These feelings maximize the potential benefit of the exercises.

Of course, breath exercises are employed not only for yoga class and meditation time. Breathing exercises with the breath cards can be used any time a child (or facilitator) is frustrated, angry, or off center or if the energy level of the entire class is escalating. The facilitator can invite a child to practice a Breath Card with a friend, the whole class, or the teacher at other times of the day. Encourage children to invent other breaths.

Benefits of Yogic Breathing

Through attention to the breath, children tap into the fullness of who they are. Greater understandings shine through with a new, fresher perspective. The mind clears. The emotions are smoother. Yogic breathing exercises can improve stress management and help overcome fear. Deeper, fuller breathing clears out stale air and improves the quantity of oxygen filling the lungs and oxygenating the entire body. When breathing is most efficient, fresh oxygen is supplied, the lungs are strengthened, and there is improved emotional stability. Children feel more self-aware and self-confident with a little less "volcanic activity" going on in the emotional body.

Pranayama directly effects the total functioning capacity of the brain and the nervous system. It supports better integration between the physical, mental, and other layers of our being. A regular pranayama practice during school time increases receptivity and focus. It improves overall oxygenation of organs and cells, calms emotions, and results in more positivity.

The Fifth Branch of Yoga:
Pratyahara, Calming the Senses

Sense withdrawal is called "Pratyahara" and provides greater calmness and self-awareness. Usually, children are very sensory occupied. Children need help in learning to withdraw attention from their senses. In yoga there are various methods to introvert the senses or calm the senses. Young children primarily learn it with the practice of Shavasana or deep relaxation. The key goal of Shavasana is to induce a state of relaxation and to withdraw from the external environment of busyness and entering a state of stillness and peace by closing the eyes, the mouth, and resting the hands and legs to relax into the Essence of our Being. It is generally practiced lying supine on the ground, but can be prone. It can be presented at the end of the asana practice and/or as meditation. Shavasana reinforces the feeling that we are more than the body, more than the intellect, more than our feelings. We are indeed spiritual beings having a physical experience.

How Is Pratyahara or Shavasana Introduced to Young Children?

In the deep relaxation position, the children lie down on their backs with arms at their side. Shavasana is beginning meditation or stillness. It is relaxing with mental alertness. Very young children may need some support calming their energy down. What kinds of experiences can the teacher include to facilitate serenity? Calming music, dimming the lights, speaking slower, whispering, speaking quieter, ringing a tiny bell, and so forth aid the children's efforts.

The deep relaxation experience can take many forms. A facilitator can read or tell a short story while children are lying down. This will help extend the time of stillness. Children can be invited to make "pictures in their heads" during short visualizations, stories, and imagery regarding some social dilemma that has been presenting itself. Visualization assists them in maintaining focus and concentration by activating several brain centers. For instance, ask the children to imagine that the clouds in the sky are filled with love (insert color) and they are pouring love down on them. The clouds are bathing their bodies with love from head to toe like a rainbow.

Simple affirmations may be whispered to support the students in achieving a relaxed and sweet state of being: I am calm. I am relaxed. I am OK. Students may repeat or not. The teacher may sing *Baba Nam Kevalam* (Love is all there is) softly over and over, play soft music, or sounds of nature. Be sure to allow a very brief time for stillness and quiet.

Deep Relaxation with Affirmation and Winding Down Movement:

Ahhhhhhh (on a long exhalation). I am calm. I am peaceful. I am happy.
Raise your foot and drop it to the ground.
Raise your other foot and drop it to the ground.
Raise your arm and drop it to the ground.

Raise your other arm and drop it to the ground.
Stick your tongue out and exhale 'ahhhhh'. Put the tongue back in your mouth.
Raise all your arms and legs and gently drop all of them to the ground.
Open your eyes and blink them three times. Then close them.
I am calm. I am peaceful. I am happy.

Deep Relaxation with Visualization:

You are sitting in the lap of Mother Nature surrounded by the light of love. The Love Light is filling you up. The light is covering your feet, your legs, your tummy, your chest, your shoulders, your arms, your hands, your neck, and your head. Your whole body is filled up with Light. You are shining like the moon at night. You are sitting in the lap of your Divine Friend who is always with you…and who will always be with you…."

Deep Relaxation Flow

During the Shavasana practice, the teacher may review points, comments, and ideas that were shared throughout the class about kindness, sharing, and gentleness. The facilitator puts an enormous focus on love and positivity. Remember that the mind is more malleable when relaxed. You may ask the children to say inside their heads (or whisper) and hearts, "I am Great. I am Good. I am Love." "We are Love. We are Light."

Initially the shavasana experience may last one to three minutes. The teacher observes the children for restlessness as to when the practice should end. Shavasana is another time to nurture their relationship with every child by gently touching the head of every child.

Some Benefits of Shavasana

Calming the senses clears the mind. Pratyahara or the Shavasana practice (which is one of the exercises of Pratyahara) clears the mind, reduces stress, supports an inner connection, magnifying the feeling of connection with that Shining Light Within. It can increase concentration, attention, and intuition.

The Sixth Branch of Yoga:
Dharana, Concentrated Meditation

A CONCENTRATED MEDITATION FLOW IS called "Dharana." In young children, Dharana is equivalent to meditation and other meditation preparations like chanting. Chanting is the rhythmic speaking or singing of words or sounds. Chanting a mantra, sacred text, name of God, or other words is a commonly used ancient practice. There are two basic types of chanting. "Japa" or "personal chanting" is when one chants alone. Chanting in a group is called "kiirtan." Kiirtan can be accompanied by musical instruments (percussion instruments that the children can play themselves), clapping, a teacher led instrumentation or using something from YouTube. It can include dance movements and gestures. Young children particularly enjoy kiirtan.

Chanting with a Mantra

Mantra is the transformation of breath into sound. This sound may be a single syllable or a group of words. Clinical studies indicate that rhythmic breathing and repetition redirect negative thinking and can bring a more positive mental focus. The actual word "mantra" means "that which liberates the mind," so using mantra has the capability of uplifting moods and minimizing negative thinking patterns. It is extremely effective in transforming and balancing the emotional well-being. Rabbi Shefa Gold said about chanting, "Chant is a bridge between the inner life and the outer expression, between the solitary practice and the shared beauty of the fellowship. When we chant, we are using the whole body as the instrument with which to feel the meaning of the sacred phrase."[1]

Many mantras are derived from the Sanskrit language. The Sanskrit alphabet is based on the inner sounds emanating from within the subtle body, specifically from the fifty glands clustered around the chakras. Advanced meditators attuned their minds to these inner sounds and each sound became one letter. There are fifty glands, fifty sounds, and subsequently fifty letters in the Sanskrit alphabet. The Sanskrit language is the human body's eternal song. The careful combination of Sanskrit letters can vibrate these glands, creating a powerful elevating effect on the mind.

Mantra is a tool that young children can use to direct the mind towards positivity. By engaging in a mantra practice, children choose the thoughts that define who they are, what they want to feel and believe. Mantra and kiirtan can be key to withdrawing the young mind from distractions and negativity. Chanting or singing mantra is a salve that heals the wound of disrupted peace during stressful times.

Chanting and Kiirtan Methodology

When singing kiirtan, the breath becomes slow and deep due to the lengthy exhalations. Consequently, many of the benefits of Pranayama, the science of breath, are applicable to chanting as both of

1

these practices have the shared benefit of relaxing the sympathetic nervous system. With a calmer mind, children make better decisions. Mental equipoise influences their feelings of peace and harmony. Children pick up on each other's finer feelings and thoughts when they are projected during chanting. This is how the world becomes a better place. Like a spiritual aspirant once said, "If one does kirtan with one's heart full of … (devotion) and … (love) even the trees, birds, and animals will respond. They will be deeply influenced. Such is the power of kiirtan. It brings the devotee face to face with God."

Chanting Techniques

With young children, chanting may be with words and/or sounds that have meaning or no meaning, simply because they like to play and explore everything, including sound. The following are a few fun chanting experiences that can be shared with children either as part of the meditation practice or during another activity:

- The vowels: Ahhhhh. AAAAA. EEEEEE. IIIIIII. OOOOOO. UUUUUU.
- Consonants: MMMMM. SSSSSSS. Shhhhhh, Shhhhhh.
- Om. (The cosmic or psychic sound of all living beings working together.)
- International words for "Peace," such as Shanti (India,) Paz (Portuguese/Spanish,) Amani (Swahili,) Salam (Eritrea.)
- International words for "Hello" such as Shalom (Israel,) Jambo (Swahili,) Aloha (Hawaii, U.S.,) Namaskar or Namaste (India,) Konichiwa (Japan.)
- Affirmational chanting, i.e., Love is above me. Love is below me. Love is all around.
- "Baba Nam Kevalam." (Love is all there is.)

The universal mantra, "Baba Nam Kevalam" (Love is all there is), is a favorite chant of children. Young children think and feel the meaning when they repeat this mantra silently or aloud. Facilitators can combine the meaning with the actual singing of the mantra. For example, "Baba Nam Kevalam. Love is all there is."

Singing the mantra prior to meditation prepares the body-mind for stillness. All of the children can sing it together, and, while they are meditating, the facilitator can continue singing it softly. The chanting melodies may range from a simple monotone to a few notes using any melody. Any tune can accompany the mantra. When singing together, children love moving their hands: clapping, holding hands, and clapping partner's hands. They enjoy waving their arms, sweeping them overhead, behind the back, and so forth. And don't forget those feet: stomping, marching, twirling, and jumping. Dance movements can also be added.

Vocalization of Mantra

There are five levels of chanting vocalization: singing loudly, singing softly, whispering, moving only the lips (no sound), and completely internalizing the sound. Let the children experiment with the five levels.

Chanting Flow

Singing chants need not occur only during meditation. One may break out into a chant at any moment during the day. It is particularly effective in changing a personal flow or the group flow when a child (or teacher) is experiencing sadness, frustration, or burnout. Chanting can also be expressed when feeling happy or joyful, or for absolutely no reason at all!

It can be practiced with young children while sitting or standing, prior to meditation, during meditation, or during deep relaxation. Experiment with chanting while a drum is played, a bell chimed, a singing bowl engaged, or other instrumentation.

Benefits of Chanting

Chants, songs, and mantras provide "technical support" for young children in directing the mind toward a specific positive goal. Through this practice we choose the positive power that certain syllables evoke.

Kabir said, "If you want the truth, I'll tell you the truth. Listen to the secret sound which is inside you. The One no one talks of…He speaks the secret sounds to Himself and He is the One who has made it all."[2]

Chanting "Baba Nam Kevalam" is a method for regaining and maintaining peace during stressful times. When a child feels stressed, five to ten minutes of focused chanting (especially external) can clear away negative thoughts that obstruct connection to Inner Harmony. Scientific studies indicate that repetition of certain sounds has a calming effect. When sad or frustrated, it can uplift the emotions and refocus the attention towards positivity. Singing "Baba Nam Kevalam", as it is a mantra of love and connection, accelerates the speed of one's momentum towards achieving that Supreme State of Balanced Being within. The mental clarity that comes from chanting can help young children to find solutions to problems and can provide relief from physical and psychic ailments.

2

The Seventh Branch of Yoga: Dhyana, Sustained Meditation

Sustained meditation is called "Dhyana". It is the touchstone for self-transformation and ongoing spiritual development. It is the practice of quieting the body and filling the mind with the highest positive Good and holding it there for a while.

How is Sustained Meditation Introduced to Young Children?

Since young children may find it difficult to focus on an idea or a point, often the "point" of focus is on sound. Yogic meditation is not emptying the mind of thoughts and maintaining a thought-free mental void. Yogic meditation is a process of guiding the thoughts and filling the mind with the Highest Good. This may be achieved in a variety of ways, but some time dedicated to mantra, the highest, subtlest of sounds, is essential. "Baba Nam Kevalam," Love is Everywhere, is a favorite.

It takes time and practice to focus the thoughts. The young mind is restless and needs something to grab onto, so having the facilitator sing or whisper "Baba Nam Kevalam" throughout the meditation can assure a more successful experience. The child's mind, thoughts, and body are further focused by visual aids (within and/or without) and with kinesthetic experiences through mudras (gestures) or holding something in their hands. Visual, auditory, and kinesthetic involvements are blended with feeling the love, feeling the light, and feeling the Goodness.

Meditation Methodology and Preparations for Meditation

As a preparation for meditation; singing, chanting, and yogic breathing can bring the unity of spirit and quieting of the mind and body. Inviting children in conversations about "What makes you happy?" or "Who loves you?" can be helpful in bringing positive feelings to their minds, hearts, and bodies which is key to yoga meditation. The facilitator may want to guide this discussion towards things that Mommy, Daddy, or friends do to make us happy rather than physical objects. The children can hold these feelings in their hearts with their hands over their chests during meditation as a reminder to "hold the feeling in your heart."

The meditation experience has to be both child-directed and teacher-directed. Children participate more readily when they are involved and are given some responsibility concerning the experience. Think about ways to give children choices so that they may participate in a more dynamic way. You may decide to choose one or two "Lead Children for the Day" to make choices about what hand position or mudra shall the group express today? How many times will the chant be repeated? Will the children sit or lie down? If seated, will the eyes be open or gazing at an object? From the facilitator's plate of nature objects, which one will be the focus of the day-- placed in the middle of the circle?

Meditation Positions

Meditation is practiced in a position comfortably held. For the very young child meditation is sometimes more effective in a lying down position which minimizes distractions. Young children are naturally conditioned to being relaxed when in a supine position on their backs. (They do not fall asleep like older kids and adults.) In the shavasana pose (supine pose) they can actually hold their meditation for much longer than when seated. However, seated meditation is beneficial of course.

Meditation Techniques

Nature objects ~ Giving each child a nature object to hold. Students may hold a shell, a stone, a pine cone, fairy or dragon tear.

Story meditation ~ Compose a very short story (fiction and/or non-fiction) children can listen to while meditating.

Bell ~ The bell guides our way to our inner home within the heart. Softly ring the bell throughout the meditation. Allow it to resonate OR ring it once at the beginning and once at the end. Have a child help you ring the bell.

Candle Gazing ~ Chant together, "I am a child of Light. I bring Light to everyone," and gaze at a candle. Notice the blue at the bottom of the flame and the brown in the middle of the flame. Can you see the wick? Look at the bright yellow part of the flame. It is warm. Repeat, "I am a child of Light. I bring Light to everyone."

Dragon Smiles ~ Each child may be holding and rubbing a glass dragon tear in one hand. Say, "Every time you rub a dragon tear with your finger, a dragon somewhere in the world smiles." (Smooth polished stones also works for this.) "What other happy things can happen in the world every time you rub the magic stone?"

Little Light of Mine ~ Invite all the children to tap lightly on their hearts and to look down at their hearts. They can say: "Touch the Light. Smile to your Light. Feel your Light. It is always shining deep in your heart even in the night." "Listen, listen, listen to my Light. It shines in my heart even in the night." Children can speak to your Light: "Hello, Little Light, are you there? Hello, Little Light, are you home?"

Rainbow ~ "Paint a picture in your mind with your eyes closed of the rainbow. Pick one color and cover your whole body in that color. Paint your body from your head to your toes in that color. How does it feel? Isn't this wonderful? It's a color shower."

Flower ~ Provide a rose (real or synthetic) or other flowers. You may get one that will be passed and shared in the class OR you may give one flower to every child. "Each one of you is like this flower – beautiful and handsome. You smell wonderful. Everyone is coming to see you, to be near you. Everyone loves you and wants to play with you. Everyone wants you to be their friend."

Singing Bowl ~ "Invite the sound of the bell." "Listen, listen, listen to your heart's song."

Meditation Flow

The length of the meditation may be very, very short in the beginning and as the children become more comfortable the time can be lengthened. It should end when they get too wiggly. For young children, four minutes can be a very long time in a group setting.

There are techniques that the facilitator can implement to extend the meditation experience. The facilitator may bring an item and place it on each child's heart while they are being still and lying down. (They will wait for you to come around to them.) "When I see that you are being still, I will place a small animal (or nature object for example) on your heart. You may touch the animal, but please keep your eyes closed. Please stay still." The facilitatory will sing "Baba Nam Kevalam" for a few minutes while placing an object on each heart.

When closing the meditation, consider a sweet song and a collective action that is performed together or individually, such as blowing out a candle and holding hands to conclude this activity and bring unity of purpose and loving to the group.

Benefits of Sustained Meditation

There are countless clinical studies on the benefits of meditation. For young children, it gives them the opportunity to enjoy the experience of stillness and calmness. It can also encourage the development of concentration, determination, and patience. Meditation engages the brain in many ways, including self-regulation. Such a practice, over time, brings mental contentment. Psychological and emotional benefits include the stimulation of imagination, memory encoding, lessening of mental storage and retrieval problems, and balancing the emotions.

The Eighth Branch of Yoga:
Blissful Samadhi or Self-Actualization

Samadhi is the result of practicing all of the other branches of Astaunga Yoga. It is the perfect state of equilibrium derived from the daily determined investment of heart, mind, and body in the performance of spiritual yoga practices. The benefits of samadhi are profound, and can manifest as a long-lasting contentment, love of others, or actual experience of the Infinite.

In yoga class any steps towards cultivating contentment, love, relaxation, and personal balance are building blocks for samadhi. It is the result of all the positive effort towards understanding the importance of self-restraint and our membership in the earth community. The meditative practices of calming the senses, concentration, and sustained meditation refine the navigational abilities of children as they journey through life. The first steps of yoga ethics and asanas constitute the foundation for samadhi, targeting children's physical, emotional and social well-being and elevating them towards self-actualization and a greater fulfillment of balance.

To help focus children towards samadhi (perfect balance and understanding), universal love is indispensable. Universal love draws upon the extension of love, affection, and reverence not only to every human being, but to all living beings. This is natural for children. The attainment of Universal Love redefines every step of Astaunga Yoga to emphasize the unity of all life.

In the world of yoga, the concept of living or being alive is not exclusively designated only to those that breathe, but includes all life (animate and inanimate) - the air, the minerals, the dirt, plants and trees, insects, beings of the air, all who walk or slither or hop on the earth, as well as those who swim and thrive in the seas. Like indigenous cultures throughout the world, Neohumanism emphasizes how humans share kinship with all created beings of our global family and strive to live in a way that demonstrates this. Every yogi strives to not intentionally harm any living being and embraces each member of the creation with benevolence. All entities are perceived as expressions of the Divine ~ the One in the Many and the Many in the One.

In meditation, children and teachers can extend this most precious treasure of unconditional love towards everyone. The children are in a collective flow like an ocean wave, moving with all living beings together in harmony. Remind children in their meditations that they are love; love is all around them. Everywhere is love. They can catch a glimpse of samadhi balance, profound universal love, the supreme equity.

By incorporating all the steps of astaunga yoga, children can understand that the aim in life is to increasingly love and care more for themselves, for those around them, and for every being. Its daily practice gives deeper meaning to and transforms the education process to something increasingly sacred. The group effort of children moving together to perform all the elements of astaunga yoga accelerates and serves every individual well towards coming closer and touching that Inner Greatness. They become Beings of Light to each other and find their own brilliance shining brightly inside themselves as they come home to the Light of the World…like a stream flowing back to the ocean …like a ray of light returning to the sun…

Part II
Let the Fun Begin!

In Part I, we introduced you to the ancient branches of Astaunga yoga. Many suggestions were offered on how to bring alive these branches into a child's life. In Part II, we invite you to fly and soar with your yoga play. There are 25 simple yoga dramas to enhance your children's and your own personal enjoyment. We hope they give you a good base to accessorize with the other yoga experiences that were provided in the earlier chapters. These included:

12 breath exercises within the Pranayama chapter.
Deep relaxation exercises are outlined in the Pratyahara chapter.
Several chanting experiences in the Dharana branch.
10 meditation experiences in the Dhyana chapter.

Following are many yoga dramas and a variety of yoga illustration for your yoga play. We encourage yoga students to build their own yoga card collection or photos from magazines, calendars, and other sources. You may even create your very own personalized yoga journal.

As you gain fluency in combining the various branches of yoga in dramatic yoga play, you may want to construct your own yoga drama compositions. These can be aimed to reflect some of the moral dilemmas that we all live through. They can highlight learning themes your children are interested in. Yoga adventures can take children around the world and to fantasy land.

In the yoga dramas, many of the yoga poses can be expressed interchangeably with various animals or plants, for instance the dog pose can express a sheep, cat, goat, or horse. Or you can turn the dog pose or cat/cow pose into an elephant, hippo, horse, or zebra pose. Children are encouraged to add the appropriate sounds and behaviors with them. With the tree poses you may emphasize a young sapling tree, winter tree, flowering spring tree, apple tree, willow, or tree-blowing-in-the-wind. A tree can become seaweed by waving the arms like floating strands. The cobra pose can be converted into a crocodile. Monkeys, gorillas, and bears are created by standing and doing creative movement and sounds. Be free to create new yoga poses. Let the sky be the limit as you explore nature, the oceans, vehicles, space, and beyond!

Children's Yoga Postures in Order of Appearance

Cobra/Snake pose	46
Turtle pose	50
Flying bird pose	53
Meditation pose	55
Dog pose	58
Deep relaxation pose	61
Grasshopper pose	64
Crescent moon pose	67
Frog pose	70
Lion pose	73
Tree pose	76
Hero/Superboy/Supergirl pose	79
Mountain pose	81
Warrior pose	85
Laughing yoga pose	88
Namaste/Namaskar warrior pose	91
Chair pose	95
Bird pose	97
Deer pose	100
Bow and Arrow pose	110
Boat pose	113
Star pose	114

Yoga Drama ~ Adventure to Africa

Storyline	Yoga Movement
We are going on Safari. We are walking in a circle, a circle, a circle.	Children make one big circle. Walk around together.
Going to Africa, Africa, Africa.	Children clap hands while walking.
It is far away, far away, far away.	Children put a hand over an eyebrow as if looking far away.
We are almost there, almost there, almost there.	Hand is moving from eyebrow to eyebrow as if wiping away sweat.
Here we are!	Jumping up in air and then down.
I see elephants walking!	Forward bend until hands and feet are on the ground.
Forward 1,2,3,4,5,6,7,8. Backward 1,2,3,4,5,6,7,8.	Everyone can walk forwards and then backwards while counting.
Let's raise our trunks up high into the air. Trumpet if you dare. Ahoo, Ahoo, Ahoo.	Interlace our fingers together and raise like trunks.
Elephants can walk bent over swinging their trunks from side to side. Swish. Swish.	Bend over and swish side to side the arms like trunks.

Storyline	Yoga Movement
Elephants can eat leaves from the trees reaching high with their trunks.	Make smacking sounds with the mouth.
Elephants can spray water on their friends	Ssshhh. Ssshhh. Ssshhh. Make sounds and move arms like spraying trunks.
Oh my goodness, the elephant has accidentally stepped on the snake. Aaaaaahhhhh!	Scream.
Snake is lying down.	Children lay down on their tummies with foreheads on the ground. Legs are out straight behind the body. Hands are palms down on either side of the neck. Pressing down on the hands, everyone raises their chests and heads up, holding the pose (not the breath) for just a moment.
All snakes hiss and hiss. They lower their bodies back to the ground.	Hiss and lower body. Tongues slither in and out of their mouths.
The elephant apologizes, "It was an accident. I'm so sorry."	
The snake says. "I forgive you since it was just an accident. You didn't mean to hurt me."	
The elephant helps to lift the snake up into the acacia tree.	Everyone stands straight and tall rooted in Mother Earth. They do tree pose by standing on one leg. Palms come together over the heart and then are lifted up, up over the head. As the arm trunks straighten, the palms open, spreading apart, like a tree branch. Children may lean against wall behind them or place one hand on the chair.

Storyline	Yoga Movement
Who else do you see in Africa	Children invent a movement that matches their animal of choice such as gorilla, lemur, hippo, zebra and crocodile. Each pose can be repeated four times with sounds or movements.
Oh, the sun is setting. It is time for everyone to find a place to sleep.	
Show me how monkeys sleep? They sleep high in the trees on a lovely branch so I want everyone to find your special branch and lie down.	Children lie on their backs with their hands on their tummies.
What sounds do you think they make as they sleep?	Breathe in and feel the tummies rise high like the mountain and as we breathe out (blowing breath), the tummies come down. Watch your hands on your tummy go up and down. Up and down. Listen to your breathing.

Meditative Moment and Relaxation

Children continue to lie on their backs and relax. Remember all the animal friends that we saw today like the elephant and snake, (continue with naming animals), and oh yes, the tree which is where we made our beds today. Imagine that you are the Elephant or the Snake. You are sleeping side by side, breathing as friends do together peacefully.

Remember all your friends with a smile. Feel the warm love of the sun surrounding you like a blanket. Remember that we all make mistakes and we come together to love each other, again and again.

Say to yourself: I love myself. I love my friends. We make mistakes together. We love together. Love is all there is. Namaste/Namaskar.

Yoga Drama ~Turtle and Rabbit Race

Storyline	Yoga Movement
Once upon a time there was a turtle and a rabbit. The turtle's movements were slow and steady. The rabbit's way was fast and soft.	
Turtle said, "I am slow. I am steady. I do not quit."	Children repeat: "I am slow. I am steady. I do not quit." Children do turtle pose. They can sing a turtle song and do turtle hand gestures by sitting and positioning one hand facing downward over the other to form the shell. Wiggle the bottom fingers to look and move like moving turtle legs and arms.
Along came Rabbit who said, "I'm fast. I'm beautiful. I'm soft." The children repeat: "I'm fast. I'm beautiful. I'm soft."	Then the children act like rabbits wiggling their noses and taking rabbit sniffs. Children can sing a rabbit song. They make "hand rabbits" with long ears, hopping along.
After Rabbit ran away from Turtle, it met Dog. Rabbit told Dog, "I am so fast I can beat Turtle in a race."	Children do dog pose. They bark and pant like a dog by putting their tongues out and panting: Heh, heh, heh.
Next, Rabbit met Snake and said, "I am so fast. I can beat Turtle in a race."	Children do snake pose and hiss. SSS.
Rabbit met other animals in the forest. To each animal, Rabbit brags.	Children can make suggestions which animals to do. Rabbit tells each animal they suggest, "I am so fast. I can beat turtle in a race."

Storyline	Yoga Movement
After some time, Rabbit said, "I am tired. (Yawning). I will sleep under this tree. Turtle is so far behind me that I can have a nice nap and still I will beat him."	Children do tree pose. Then children yawn and make sleeping sounds. They lie down to sleep.
While Rabbit was sleeping, slowly, ever so slowly, Turtle walked by. As it walked by Rabbit, Turtle said, "I am slow. I am steady. I do not quit." Slowly, Turtle neared the end of the race. Just as it was almost to the winning line, Turtle repeated, "I am slow. I am steady. I do not quit."	The children repeat, "I am slow. I am steady. I do not quit." They walk turtle-style in slow motion. Still walking like turtles in slow motion, children repeat, "I am slow. I am steady. I do not quit."
Suddenly, Rabbit woke up and saw Turtle. It tried to run very fast and win, but, sadly, it could not. Turtle said, "I am slow. I am steady. I do not quit. Slow and steady wins the race!"	The children repeat, "I am slow. I am steady. I do not quit. Slow and steady wins the race!"

Meditative Moment and Relaxation

Children sit and put one hand on top of the other hand in their laps. Imagine inside your hands is sitting the winning turtle. Try to see its little head and feet sticking out of its shell. Hear the turtle say to you: "Be steady. Do not quit." Repeatedly say this in a slow and prolonged voice.

Rabbit and Turtle relaxed after their race. Like Rabbit and Turtle, let's massage ourselves. "First, give yourself a big hug. Rub your head, face, chest, arms, legs, and feet. Lie down and do balloon breath--breathe in and push the tummy up to let the air fill it like it fills a balloon. Breathe out and lower your tummy to let the air out."

"Please close your eyes and relax." While they relax, let it be silent, do a guided imagery or play music. After a long pause, ask the children to wiggle and stretch.

"You were absolutely awesome in yoga play today. We will end yoga play with Namaste/Namaskar. Breathe in and raise your arms up over head, palms together, bring them to forehead and heart while saying Namaste/Namaskar."

Teaching Tips

Add any turtle song such as "There was a Little Turtle" or "I had a Little Turtle" as well as any rabbit song like "Little Bunny Foo Foo". Homemade yoga cards from magazines, the internet, calendars, and books can help the children choose poses. Other forest animals can include: fox, bear, fish, squirrel, deer and other indigenous forest animals. Make up poses for these.

Yoga Drama ~ Black Bird Gives the Best Present

Storyline	Yoga Movement
Once upon a time, there was a baby Black Bird who wanted to give a present to its mother. It wanted to give the best present in the whole world.	Children do a bird pose. Let's make the sound of blackbirds, "Caw, caw."
Black Bird needs a little help on what present to give. It flies to the wise tree and asks Tree, "What is the best present to give my mother?"	Some children fly like the Black Bird to other children who are doing the tree pose.
Tree says, "I like to give nuts. Give your mother nuts."	Children roll around on the floor like nuts.
Black Bird says, "No, mother does not want that." Then Black Bird flies to Turtle and asks, "What is the best present to give my mother?"	Wave their finger side to side, indicating no. Children do the turtle pose.
Turtle says, "I like to give seaweed. Give your mother seaweed."	Children stand and wave their arms like seaweed waving in the ocean.
Blackbird says, "No, mother does not want that."	Children wave their finger side to side, indicating no.
Black Bird goes to Rabbit and asks, "What is the best gift to give my mother?"	Children act like a rabbit and do rabbit sniffs.
Rabbit says, "I like to give carrots. Give your mother carrots." Blackbird says, "No, mother does not want that."	Children wave their finger side to side, indicating no.
Black Bird asks other animals, "What is the best gift for my mother?"	Each time the animals suggest something, the children do their poses.
Black Bird says every time, "No, mother does not want that." Black Bird was very sad. None of the suggestions sounded like the best present in the world.	Children wave their finger side to side, indicating no. Children look sad.
Black Bird sits down and closes his eyes. He looks inside his heart and finds the best present for his mother.	All children sit down cross-legged and close their eyes in a meditative moment.

Storyline	Yoga Movement
Black Bird opens his eyes and smiles.	Children open their eyes and smile. Ask the children what is the best gift to give their mothers or dear ones. All their answers are acceptable.
Black Bird said, "Mothers like hugs and love. That is the best present in the whole wide world. I will give her a big hug."	"Let's give ourselves a big hug like we would hug our mothers or dear ones. Rub your head, face, chest, arms, legs, and feet."

Relaxation Moment

Children lie down. They are invited to do the balloon breath. Children close their eyes and relax. After a long pause, ask the children to wiggle and stretch. Tell the children, "You were awesome in yoga play. Namaste/Namaskar."

Yoga Drama ~ Magic Cat

Storyline	Yoga Movement
Once upon a time, there was a Magic Cat. The cat sang (in a singsong voice), "I'm a Magic Cat. I'm sassy and fat. And I can change who I am (snap fingers) just like that. I can become a dog."	Children do the dog pose, do dog behaviors, and bark.
After becoming a dog, the Magic Cat wanted to be something else. "I'm a Magic Cat, I'm sassy and fat. And I can change who I am (snap fingers) just like that. "I can become a tree."	Children do tree pose, waving their leaves.
After becoming a tree, the Magic Cat wanted to move more because the tree was too still. "I'm a Magic Cat, I'm sassy and fat. And I can change who I am (snap fingers) just like that. I can become a frog."	Children do frog pose. They jump around and make frog sounds.
After becoming a frog, the Magic Cat still wanted to be another animal and it sang, "I'm a Magic Cat, I'm sassy and fat. And I can change who I am (snap fingers) just like that. I can become a ...."	Children can perform various poses like bird, bear, and others. Each time in a singsong voice the Magic Cat sings its magic song to introduce the new animal.
After Magic Cat became so many animals, it sang, "I'm a Magic Cat, I'm sassy and fat. And I can change who I am (snap fingers) just like that. I just want to be me, the Magic Cat. And, Magic Cat is what I will be." And Magic Cat curled up to sleep.	Children do cat pose, they mew, and they make cat sounds. Then curl up to sleep.

Meditative Moment and Relaxation

Ask the children to purr like a cat. People purr by humming. Have the children sing a drawn out "Hum" together. Then ask them to close their eyes, cover their ears with their palms, and listen to themselves hum. Ask the children to chant "Om".

Let's massage ourselves like the Magic Cat. First, hug yourself. Rub your head, face, chest, arms, legs, and feet. Lie down and do balloon breath. Close your eyes and relax. While they relax, let it be silent, do guided imagery or play music. After a long pause, ask the children to wiggle and stretch.

"You were awesome in yoga play. We will end yoga play with Namaste/Namaskar. Breathe in and raise your arms up over head, palms together, bring them to forehead and heart while saying Namaste/Namaskar."

Yoga Drama ~ A New Sound

(This drama needs a singing bowl, large bell, cymbals or an unusual instrument to play.)

Storyline	Yoga Movement
Once upon a time, there were little children and they wanted a new sound. "We need a new sound. Let us ask Cat for a new sound." The cat meowed for the children.	Do cat pose. Move around like the cat. Make cat sounds.
"Is the cat sound a new sound?" asked the children. "No, that's not a new sound."	Children wave their finger from side to side to indicate "no".
"Let's ask Donkey for a new sound." The donkey brayed for the children.	Children act like a donkey by lifting one back leg and then the other. They bray or heehaw and move around like donkeys.
"Is the donkey sound a new sound?" asked the children. "No. That's not a new sound."	Children wave their finger from side to side to indicate "no".
"Let's ask .... for a new sound?"	Invite children to suggest animals. Do their poses and make sounds.
But each time after they heard the animal's sound, the children said, "No. That's not a new sound."	Each time ask children, "Is that a new sound?" and prompt children to reply, "No. That's not a new sound."
"Let's ask a Rabbit for a new sound. Let's all be rabbits."	Children act like a rabbit. They sniff, wiggle their noses, and hop like rabbits.

Storyline	Yoga Movement
Rabbit says, "I have a new sound. I have a new instrument and I will play it for you." The children had not heard it before. "That is a new sound," they said.	Play a singing bowl/bell/cymbals or an unusual instrument for them. Ask all the children to sit in a circle. Play the instrument for them and listen to the sound. Go, one by one, to each child in the circle. Help each child try out the instrument. Say to each child, "You made a new sound."

Meditative Moment and Relaxation

A meditative moment can be created by asking the children to close their eyes and listen to the sound of the singing bowl or another unusual instrument or play a recording of it from a phone app or computer site.

After listening, ask the children to: "Give yourself a big hug." Children rub their head, face, chest, arms, legs, and feet. Lie down and do balloon breath. They close their eyes.

While they relax, let it be silent, do a guided imagery or play music. After a long pause, ask the children to wiggle and stretch.

"You were awesome in yoga play. We will end yoga play with Namaste/Namaskar. Breathe in and raise your arms up over head, palms together, bring them to your forehead and heart while saying Namaste/Namaskar."

Teaching Tips

Other animals to act out are are bears, wolves, crows, squirrel, mountain lions, eagles, buffalos, owls or other indigenous animals. Homemade cards of the animals are helpful. Cards can be face down to create suspense or faced up.

This story can also be done with dinosaurs. Children can make up dinosaur movements and sounds for each dinosaur.

Yoga Drama ~ Birthday Cake Play

Storyline	Yoga Movement
Once upon a time, there was a dog who was going to have a birthday. "Are any of you having a birthday soon?"	Listen to their responses. Do the dog pose with the children. Move around like dogs. "What do dogs say?"
Dog wanted to make a big cake for her birthday party. She wanted her friends to help her make a birthday cake. "I will ask my friends to make a cake with me," Dog said. So Dog met her friend Cat.	Children do cat pose, cat sounds and make cat movements. Let them pretend to be cats chasing their tails and spin around.
Dog asked Cat, "Will you make a cake with me?" But Cat said, "No, I cannot. I am going to chase mice."	Children add mouse movements and sounds. Some children can be cats and others act like mice. The cats chase mice carefully.
Dog went to her friend Bird and asked, "Will you make a cake with me?" But Bird said, "No, I cannot. I am busy building my nest."	Children do bird pose and flap around.
Dog went to her friend Deer and asked, "Deer will you make a cake with me?" But Deer said, "No, I cannot. I am busy practicing my leaping."	The children do the deer pose and leap like deers.
Dog went to her friend ……… and asked, "…… will you make a cake with me?" But each time, the animal said, "No, I cannot. I am busy with ……"	Let children suggest other animals and do the poses and movements of the animals. Poses can be made up if you do not know the pose suggested.
Finally, Dog went home and began baking a cake by herself. She sang a baking song: "This is the way I stir the flour, stir the flour, stir the flour. This is the way I stir the flour so early in the morning. This is the way I add the butter…..This is the way I stir the batter…..This is the way I bake a cake."	Children sing and pantomime song.

59

Storyline	Yoga Movement
Then Dog put the cake in the oven.	Children lie down on the floor to 'bake', pretending to sunbathe. They smile when they feel the warm sun.
When the cake was done baking, it was time for the birthday party. Dog's friends smelled the cake.	Children pretend to smell the cake.
Cat, Bird, and Deer smelled the cake. All the animals went as fast as they could to Dog's house. They wanted to eat the delicious smelling cake.	Children get up. Some of the children can be Cat running, Bird flying, Deer leaping or any other kind of animal. All go to Dog's house.
When all the friends reached Dog's house, they sang,	"Happy birthday to you. Happy birthday to you. Happy birthday, dear Dog. Happy birthday to you."
After the birthday party, the friends gave each other a hug.	All hug.

Meditative Moment and Relaxation

Create a meditative moment by asking the children: "Close your eyes and make a wish. Keep silent and make a long, big wish. Picture the wish you are asking. Put up one finger as if it's a candle and blow it out." The children repeat these actions.

After the birthday party, the friends wanted to rest. They gave each other a hug. "Give yourself a big hug. Rub your head, face, chest, arms, legs, and feet. Lie down and do balloon breath." Ask the children to close their eyes. While they relax, let it be silent, do guided imagery or play music. After a long pause, ask the children to wiggle and stretch.

"You were awesome in yoga play. We will end yoga play with Namaste/Namaskar. Breathe in and raise your arms up over head, palms together, bring them to your forehead and heart while saying Namaste/Namaskar."

Yoga Drama ~ Mary's Little Lamb

Storyline	Yoga Movement
Once upon a time there was a little girl named Mary and she had a little lamb. Let's sing Mary's song: Mary had a little lamb, little lamb, little lamb. Mary had a little lamb its fleece was white as snow. Everywhere that Mary went, Mary went, Mary went. Everywhere that Mary went the lamb was sure to go.	Children sing the song. Then they do sheep/dog pose and make sheep sounds.
Mary looked for her little lamb. "Oh, no, my lamb is lost. Where is my little lamb?" cried Mary. "Help me find my little lamb!"	The children stand and put their hands above their eyes to shade them as if they are looking far away. They look for the lamb to the left, right, up and down. Go around the room and look.
The children meet Cat and ask, "Do you know where Mary's little lamb is?" Cat says, "MEOW. I do not know where the little lamb is. Maybe Dog knows." The children go to meet Dog and ask, "Do you know where Mary's little lamb is?"	Do cat poses. They arch and lower their back, meow and do other cat things like eat, drink, argue, hunt, purr, and sleep. Children do dog poses, wag their tails, curl up, sniff, run in a circle, catch something, and bark like a dog.
Dog says, "Ruff. Ruff. I do not know where the little lamb is. Maybe some of the other neighbors know." So, the children ask other animals.	Children walk with giant steps in Warrior pose. Children ask other animals, saying, "Do you know where Mary's little lamb is?" Each time the children do the animals' behaviors and pose.
The last animal says, "You should go ask Wise Tree. It will know.	Children do a pose for the last animal.

Storyline	Yoga Movement
The children find Wise Tree. They ask, "Do you know where Mary's lamb is?" Tree says, "Look behind my trunk and you will find the little lamb fast asleep." The children find the lamb and bring it back to Mary. She gives the lamb a big hug.	Children do tree pose, standing upright against the wall, being crooked tree, swaying from side to side with the wind, twinkling their leaves, etc Children pretend to be the sleeping lamb. They do baby pose as sleeping baby/lamb pose. Hugs all around.

Meditative Moment and Relaxation

A meditative moment can be created by placing a cotton ball in each of their hands, and asking them to touch it to their face. Is it soft like Mary's Lamb? Ask the children to close their eyes while holding the cotton in their hands.

"You are safe when you close your eyes. Imagine that around you, the air is soft like cotton, and inside your breath is soft like cotton. You are safe right now sitting here. Everything is soft. You are surrounded by softness." Eyes are closed. After a silent pause, ask the children to open their eyes.

After Mary found the little lamb, she needed to relax. Like Mary hugging the little lamb, give yourself a big hug. Then children rub their head, face, chest, arms, and close their eyes and relax. While they relax, let it be silent, do guided imagery or play music. After a long pause, ask the children to wiggle and stretch.

Tell the children, "You were awesome in yoga play. We will end yoga play with Namaste/Namaskar. Breathe in and raise your arms up over head, palms together, bring them to your forehead and heart while saying Namaste/Namaskar."

Yoga Drama ~ The Butterfly's Fun

Storyline	Yoga Movement
Once upon a time there was a little, blue butterfly who loved to fly and sing. Butterfly's favorite song was: Fly, fly, fly, the butterfly. In the garden it's flying high. In the meadow it's flying low. Fly, fly, fly, the butterfly.	Children do a bird pose and call it butterfly pose. They flutter hands and arms like a butterfly.
Often Butterfly would flutter and fly to a nearby flower.	Children butterfly their legs with their soles together, flapping their knees, and do lotus pose.
Then Butterfly saw Dog and flew to it. Butterfly landed on Dog's back. But when Dog saw Butterfly on its back; it gave a shake, shake, shake.	Children do dog pose. They bark like a dog and wag their hips like a dog wag its tail. Shake their bodies.
Butterfly flew off. It flittered over to Grasshopper.	Children do grasshopper pose.
Butterfly said to Grasshopper, "I will fly and you jump to that tree. Let's see who gets there first." Then Butterfly and Grasshopper raced to the tree. Butterfly won as flying is faster than jumping.	Children butterfly legs. They flutter their wings and run around the room. Children do grasshopper pose and hop like them. .
Hummingbird saw Butterfly and Grasshopper race. It said to Butterfly, "Try to beat me to that tree over there. So, Hummingbird and Butterfly flew quickly to the tree. Hummingbird beat Butterfly in that race.	Children do butterfly a sparrow/ hummingbird pose.
After the race, Butterfly wanted a rest so it flew away from there and landed on a snake. Snake did not want Butterfly on its back. So, Snake slithered into a hole in the ground to make Butterfly fly away.	Children do cobra pose and make a hissing sound

Storyline	Yoga Movement
Then Butterfly flew over to Cat and landed on its back. Butterfly liked how soft Cat felt. But Cat did a big stretch and Butterfly flew off.	Children do cat pose and stretch. They say, "Meow."
Just then, Butterfly saw Turtle and landed on its shell. When Butterfly landed on Turtle, Turtle stuck its head and legs inside its shell. Turtle did not move. Butterfly thought, "You aren't fun." So, Butterfly flew off and landed on Lion's head. Lion's loud roar scared Butterfly who by now was very tired. It wanted to go home.	Children do turtle pose with their bodies and/or turtle hands. Children do lion pose and roar like a lion.
And so, Butterfly flew to a small tree which was its home. Butterfly closed its eyes and napped on a leaf of the tree.	Children do tree pose. Then sleeping butterfly pose/child pose.
After a few moments Butterfly opened its eyes. Butterfly was happy after its safe, quick nap. Butterfly gave the children a butterfly hug.	Ask the children to give themselves a big hug.

Meditative Moment and Relaxation

Ask the children to sit with their palms upwards in their laps. They close their eyes and imagine a soft butterfly sleeping in their hands. "Butterfly wants to nap in your hands so it would feel safe."

Tell them to not move and sit very still. Otherwise, the butterfly will wake up.

Then children rub their head, face, chest, arms, legs, and feet. Children lie down and do balloon breath, close their eyes, and relax. After a long pause, ask the children to wiggle and stretch. "You were awesome in yoga play. Namaste/Namaskar."

Yoga Drama ~ Bat's Night Friends

Storyline	Yoga Movement
Once upon a time, there was a brown bat.	Show a picture of a bat, sleeping in a tree. Children stand with arms wrapped around them like a bat sleeping in the tree. Do bird/bat pose.
Bat liked to sleep in the day and to play at night. At night when Bat awoke it went to visit the crickets to hear them chirp.	Children do grasshopper/cricket pose and make cricket sounds.
That night had a crescent moon and the moon shone on Bat's wings. Bat loved the moon and the glow it casted.	Children do the crescent moon pose.
Then Bat watched a cat trying to catch a spider.	Children do cat pose and meow like cats. Children move their hands like spiders.
Bat saw a wolf and it was howling at the moon.	Children howl like a wolf. Then they do dog/wolf pose.
Bat was attracted to candlelight shining in a window.	Children lie on their backs and stick their legs up in the air like candles or do shoulder stand.
Bat flew to the candle glowing in the window and saw a baby sleeping while its mama hummed a lullaby.	Sing a lullaby or hum a song. Children do baby pose.
But the baby's mama saw Bat and said, "Shoo". Then Bat flew away.	Children fly and flap their wings like bats.
Bat enjoyed the creatures of the night but it was getting lighter. Morning was dawning. The sun was waking up. Bat flew to a nearby tree which was Bat's home. Bat hung upside down and went to sleep.	Children do sleeping-bat pose once more by wrapping their arms around their bodies.

Meditative Moment and Relaxation

A meditative moment can be created by the teacher holding a battery-operated candle or, with care, a lit candle. Children sit and stare at the lighted candle. Invite the children, "Close your eyes and try to see the candle burning inside your heart."

The teacher repeatedly chants or sings, "Baba nam kevalam. Love is all there is."

Then the children give themselves a big hug. Next, they rub their head, face, chest, arms, legs, and feet. Ask the children to lie down and do balloon breath. Teacher continues to chant to the resting children, "Baba nam kevalam. Love is all there is." After a long pause, ask the children to wiggle and stretch. At the end tell the children, "You were awesome in yoga play."

Yoga Drama ~ Rabbit's Big Sneeze

Storyline	Yoga Movement
Once upon a time, there was a rabbit who had a cold. It would sneeze, "AAHCHOO!"	Children pretend they are sneezing, "AACHOO." Remind them to cover their nose. They do three quick sniffs for rabbit breath, hop around, and wiggle their noses like a rabbit. They sneeze into their elbow.
Rabbit decided to go to his friends and ask them for help. First Rabbit met Bird. Rabbit asked Bird, "How do you cure a cold?"	Children do bird pose.
Bird said, "I like to ruffle my feathers and put my head down and sleep. When I wake up, my cold is better." Just then Rabbit gave a big "AACHOO" and scared Bird away.	Children pretend they are sneezing, "AACHOO". They practice sneezing into their elbow.
Next Rabbit went to Dog and asked, "How do you cure a cold?"	Children do dog pose, bark like a dog, and wag their hips like a dog wag's its tail.
Dog told Rabbit, "I like to eat a bone, then my cold is better." Rabbits do not like bones, so it hopped away.	Children do rabbit hopping.
Rabbit saw Frog and asked, "How do you cure a cold?"	Children do frog pose with their bodies and jump like frogs. They croak "RIBBIT."
Frog was about to tell Rabbit how it cured a cold, but suddenly Rabbit gave another big "AACHOO" and scared Frog. Quickly, Frog hopped away to hide.	Children pretend they are sneezing, "AACHOO" in their elbow. They do child's pose but cover their head like their hiding.

71

Storyline	Yoga Movement
Rabbit saw a little girl sitting in a chair under a tree. Rabbit asked, "How do you cure a cold?" The little girl said, "My Mama makes me take a nap. When I wake up my cold is better."	Children do the chair pose.
Rabbit thought this was a great idea, but suddenly Rabbit gave a big, "AACHOO". The sneeze scared the little girl away.	Children pretend they are sneezing, "AACHOO" in their elbow. Then run in a circle.
Next, Rabbit went to Tree and asked, "How do you cure a cold?" Tree said, "I do not get colds."	Children do tree pose.
So Rabbit looked for someone else to ask. Rabbit spied Snake and asked, "How do you cure a cold?"	Children do cobra pose and hiss.
Snake said "I lie in the sun. When my body gets all warmed up, my cold is better." Rabbit liked Snake's suggestion. Rabbit went over to some nice tall grass and laid down in the sun. The sun felt warm and cozy. Rabbit's cold felt better.	Children do star pose. They make an "X" shape with their bodies. They are the star/sun. Invite them to shine light everywhere. Spread their toes and fingers to shine brighter.
"The sun has cured my cold!" Rabbit cheered.	Everyone twinkles their fingers and cheers, too!

Meditative Moment and Relaxation

To create a meditative moment, ask the children to sit and close their eyes. Imagine the sun is shining down. "Pretend you feel the warm sunshine all over. You can feel its light and feel the warmth of the sun on your skin. It is warming your entire body."

Invite the children to give themselves a big hug. They rub their head, face, chest, arms, legs, and feet. Lie down, do balloon breath, and relax. Teacher sings, "Baba nam kevalam ~ Love is all there is." After a long pause, ask the children to wiggle and stretch. "You were awesome in yoga.

Yoga Drama ~ Where Has My Little Dog Gone?

Storyline	Yoga Movement
Once upon a time, there was a brown dog that the children loved. One day the dog was lost. The children sang this song. Oh, where oh where has my little dog gone? Oh, where oh where can it be? With its ears quite long and its tail quite short. Oh, where oh were can it be?	Children do the dog pose and bark like dogs. They can do happy barks. Children show how does a happy dog move its tail and sway their hips. They switch to mean dogs and make barks and growls. Ask the children to show their teeth like a mad dog.
The children miss their dog so they go searching for it. They meet a turtle and ask, "Do you know where our little dog has gone?"	The children put their hands over their brows as they search with giant Warrior steps. They do turtle pose.
Turtle says, "No, I do not know where the little dog has gone." The children go meet a lion and ask, "Do you know where my little dog has gone?"	Children do lion pose and roar. They make happy lion and anxious lion faces.
Lion says, "No, I do not know where the little dog has gone." The children ask _____ (they suggest animals to ask.) Each time the various animals say, "I do not know where the little dog has gone."	Children do various animal poses. Do the pose and movement of each animal a child suggests.
Finally, the children go to a big tree. The big tree points with a branch to look behind at the tree's base.	Children do the tree pose.
At the tree's base, curled into a ball, the children found their little dog fast asleep. "Our dog has been found," the children shouted. "Yay!"	They do sleeping baby pose.

Meditative Moment and Relaxation

A meditative moment can be created by asking the children to stick out their tongues and pant like a dog. "Can you touch your tongue to the top of the mouth? Now put your tongues away. " You may have to demonstrate.

Invite the children to close their eyes and feel their tongue sitting in the mouth. "Keep closing your eyes and feeling your tongue." After a silent pause, let them open their eyes.

"After finding the little dog, the children wanted to rest. First, they gave themselves a big hug. Children rub their head, face, chest, arms, legs, and feet. "Please lie down and do balloon breath."

While they relax, let there be silence or play music. After a long pause, ask the children to wiggle and stretch.

"You were awesome in yoga play. We will end yoga play with Namaste/Namaskar. Breathe in and raise your arms up over head, palms together. Bring them to your forehead and heart while saying Namaste/Namaskar."

Yoga Drama ~ Baby Crocodile Play

Storyline	Yoga Movement
Once upon a time there was a baby crocodile. It was stuck in some mud and needed help. Can we help the Baby Crocodile?	Children do crocodile/cobra pose, smacking arms or legs together to make its mouth.
We need some strong animals to help crocodile. Let us ask lion. "Lion can you help Baby Crocodile get out of the mud?"	Then children do lion pose.
Lion roared and said, "I can help." Lion tried to pull Baby Crocodile out of the mud, but Lion could not.	Children pretend to pull. And pull while roaring.
Children ask other African animals to help get Baby Crocodile out of the mud, "Can you help Baby Crocodile get out of the mud?" Each animal tries to pull Baby Crocodile out of the mud, but it cannot.	The children suggest animals. They do a pose for each of the animals suggested.
Then the last animal says, "If all the animals pulled together, we could free Baby Crocodile."	Every animal pantomimes pulling Baby Crocodile out of the mud, but it cannot.
Baby Crocodile says, "You need a stick to pull me out." The animals walked to a nearby tree and ask the tree, "Can we please have a branch to pull Baby Crocodile out of the mud?"	Do crocodile poses.
Tree says, "I want to help. Here take this nice long, strong branch.	Children do tree pose.

Storyline	Yoga Movement
The animals take the strong branch. They all held on to one end and Baby Crocodile took the other end.	Give the children a rope and play a tug of war game or pull waist of child in front. On one side are the crocodiles and the other side are the various animals.
Then they pulled and pulled. Little by little, Baby Crocodile moved through the mud until it was free.	Another option is to bring a good stick and let children, one by one, try to pull it from the adult's hand.
The animals said, "Hurray!"	
"Thank you," says Baby Crocodile to all the animals. It wiped off some of the mud caked to its body and crawled into the water.	Children rub their heads, face, chest, arms, legs, and feet, getting the mud off their bodies. Then they lie down on their tummies like baby crocodiles swimming in the water.
Baby Crocodile went swimming away to look for food. What food did it find?	Children lie on their sides and make their arms (or legs) open and close like a crocodile's mouth.
Baby Crocodile ate a banana. Then it hid under the water. But, still it needed more food. The Baby Crocodile opened its mouth and another food dropped in it.	Chomp, goes the arms/legs-mouth and the banana is eaten. Then they lie down to hide under the water. Ask the children, "What else do they want to eat?" Each time, the children open and close their arms/legs-mouth and lie down again to swim under the water.
After enjoying, the crodile hid back under the water.	
Now Baby Crocodile was full. It swam to a log and lay its head on it and took a long nap.	Baby Crocodiles swim back under the water. Then pillow their heads and pretend to sleep.

Meditative Moment and Relaxation

Children imagine they are sitting in a warm bath tub, feeling safe and cozy. Invite them to close their eyes and feel the warm water around them.

While they relax, let them be silent. Teacher sings, "Baba nam kevalam ~ Love is all there is." Do guided imagery or play music. After a long pause, ask them to wiggle and stretch.

"You were awesome in yoga play. We will end yoga play with Namaste/Namaskar. Breathe in and raise your arms up over head, palms together. Bring them to your forehead and heart. Namaste/Namaskar."

Yoga Drama ~ Jungle Play

Storyline	Yoga Movement
Once upon a time the children wanted to go to the jungle. "Going to the jungle. Going to the jungle." They rhythmically clap their thighs.	Let the children sit in a circle and chant, "Going to the jungle." They repeat this over and over.
The children walked around. They knew many animals lived in the jungle.	Children walk in Warriorlike giant strides.
As they walk in a circle, they sing a walking song. "Walking thru the jungle. Walking thru the jungle. What do you see? What do you see? I think I see a _____." (Children name an animal.)	Ask the children, "What other animal is in the jungle?" Children do the animal pose suggested and mimic its behaviors.
They walk deeper into the jungle. Again, they sing the walking song. "Walking thru the jungle. Walking thru the jungle. What do you see? What do you see? I think I see a _____. (Children name an animal.)	Children suggest more animals to meet in the jungle. They do their poses and behaviors.
Finally, the children are ready to leave the jungle. To each of the jungle animals, they sing, "Good-bye _____."	As they say goodbye, they re-enact each animal.

Meditative Moment and Relaxation

Children sit and close their eyes. "Draw a picture of a jungle animal in your mind. What's it like in the jungle today? Now, open your eyes and tell everyone what animal you saw."

"Close your eyes and draw a picture in your mind of someone you love." After a silent pause, ask the children to open their eyes. "Who did you see?" Suggest to the children that when they meet that person to give him or her a big hug. Now ask the children to hug themselves. Stroke their head, face, chest, arms, legs, and feet. Then children lie down and do balloon breath. The children close their eyes and relax. After a suitable pause, the children may wiggle and stretch. Tell them, "You were awesome in yoga play."

Yoga Drama ~ Bear Over the Mountain Play

Storyline	Yoga Movement
Once upon a time, there was a bear who wanted to visit his grandma. But he did not know where she lived.	Ask the children, "Do you have a grandpa or grandma?" After they respond say, "A young bear wanted to visit his grandma." Make a sound like a bear. Make a pose like a bear walking on all four limbs.
Bear's grandma lived somewhere on the mountain. The mountain was too big to search for her without an address. So Bear thought, "I must ask someone where my grandma lives." Bear saw Bird and asked, "Do you know where my grandma lives?"	Children stand like a mountain. Do bird pose.
Bird says, "Tweet-tweet. I do not know. The mountain is too high. Go home." But Bear responds, "I am brave. I do not give up."	Children repeat the affirmation: "I am brave. I do not give up." Children do the brave warrior pose.
Then Bear sees Rabbit hiding in the nearby bushes. Bear calls to Rabbit, "Do you know where my grandma lives?" Rabbit tells Bear, "I do not know where your grandma lives. The mountain is too high. Go home." But Bear says, "I am brave. I do not give up."	Children do rabbit's nose by wiggling their noses. Do rabbit sniffs and rabbit pose.
Bear sees a Mountain Lion. Bear asks, "Do you know where my grandma lives?"	Children do lion pose and roar like lions.
Mountain Lion tells Bear, "I do not know where your grandma lives. The mountain is too steep and you can fall. Go home." Bear says, "I am brave. I do not give up."	Ask the children to repeat, "I am brave. I do not give up."

Storyline	Yoga Movement
Bear asks other animals. Each animal says, "I do not know where your grandma lives. The mountain is too high. Go home."	Ask the children to suggest other animals to ask. Children do their poses and sounds.
Bear answers, "I am brave. I do not give up."	Children repeat, "I am brave. I do not give up."
The last animal Bear meets is Mountain Goat. Bear knows that Mountain Goat knows where everyone lives on the mountain.	Children make a goat pose by sitting on their knees. Then they buck their head like a goat with horns and shake the head like a goat.
Mountain Goat has large, curved horns and likes to stand on big rocks. Bear walks over to Mountain Goat and asks, "Do you know where my grandma lives?"	They say, "NAY" like a goat.
	Children repeat, "I am brave. I do not give up."
Mountain Goat says, "On the mountain top is a large tree. Your grandma lives by the tall tree. The mountain is too high. You should not try. Go home."	
But Bear answers, "I am brave. I do not give up."	
Then Bear starts to climb up the mountain.	Children do a climbing action.
Bear gets tired of climbing, but Bear says, "I am brave. I do not give up."	Children continue to do climbing actions. They repeat, "I am brave. I do not give up."
Bear climbs higher and higher. His legs become even more tired. But Bear again says, "I am brave. I do not give up."	Children do tree pose.
Finally, Bear reaches the top of the mountain and sees Tall Tree.	
Behind the tree, Bear finds his grandma and gives her a big bear hug. They sit together to rest after Bear's climb. They close their eyes and feel the vastness around them on top of the mountain.	Ask the children to sit with their eyes closed and feel like they are on top of the mountain. Feel the vastness around them. There is a gentle breeze on their faces. "Can you feel the breeze on your face?" Give a long meditative pause.
Grandma was so happy to be with Bear. She gave Bear a big hug and said, "I love you. You were so brave to climb up here."	Children give themselves a big hug. They repeat "I love you. I am brave. I do not give up."
Bear said, "I love you, too, And I am brave. I do not give up."	

Meditative Moment and Relaxation

First hug yourself like your grandma or grandpa hugs you. Children stroke their head, face, chest, arms, legs, and feet. They lie down and do balloon breath. Invite the children to close their eyes and relax. Teacher sings, "Baba nam kevalam ~ Love is all there is." After a long pause, invite the children to wiggle and stretch. "You were awesome in yoga play. Namaste/Namaskar."

Yoga Drama ~ The Friendly Monkey

Storyline	Yoga Movement
Once upon a time, there was a young monkey who was very friendly. One day the monkey's mom gave Monkey a bunch of bananas to take to a friend's house. As Monkey walked to the friend's house, Monkey met many animals.	Children imitate a monkey and make monkey sounds and do behaviors.
The first animal Monkey met on her way was Rabbit. Rabbit saw the yummy bunch of bananas that Monkey carried.	Children do rabbit pose and rabbit nose. They sniff like rabbit.
Rabbit told Monkey, "I would like a banana. Can I have a banana, please?" Monkey answered, "You can have just one banana."	Do monkey movements. Children put up one finger and say, "Just one banana."
Monkey walked further and met another animal. (Let the children suggest the next animal to meet.) Each animal says, "I would like a banana. Can I have a banana, please?" Monkey answers, "You can have just one banana."	Children take giant Warrior Steps. Do the suggested animal's pose and sound. Each animal says, "Can I have a banana, please?" The children repeat, "Just one banana."
Finally, Monkey has only two bananas left. When Monkey reached her friend, she said, "I have one banana for you and one for me." "Thank you," said her friend and she gave Monkey a big hug.	Everyone hugs and says "Namaste/Namaskar."

Meditative Moment and Relaxation

The children put their hands in "Namaste/Namaskar" pose at their hearts and close their eyes. Tell them to think of one person they would like to share bananas with like the monkey did. After a long meditative pause, the children open their eyes. Ask them to give themselves a big hug.

86

Children rub their head, face, chest, arms, legs, and feet. They lie down and do balloon breath. Invite the children to close their eyes and relax. After a long pause ask the children to wiggle and stretch.

"You were awesome in yoga play. Let's share a Namaste/Namaskar with each other." Everyone shares a panoramic Namaste/Namaskar by gliding the gesture from left to right until they have given their Namaste/Namaskar to everyone present.

Yoga Drama ~ The Funny Goose

Storyline	Yoga Movement
Once upon a time, there was a sad princess who would not laugh. The princess only frowned. She did not laugh.	Ask the children to make a big frown.
The King, her father, wanted her to laugh. He told everyone in the kingdom, "If anyone can make the princess laugh, I will give them a bag of gold." Many tried but could not make her laugh. One boy said, "I will bring my goose to her. It's a funny goose and may make her laugh."	Children do bird pose and call it goose pose. Children make the sound of a goose, "Honk. Honk." And waddle together in a single file line like geese.
While the boy and goose walked to the palace, they met a dog.	Children do the dog pose and bark like the dog and wag their hips like a dog's tail.
The dog liked the funny goose and boy. So, the dog began to follow them. After a while, the boy, goose, and dog met a cat. The cat liked the boy and funny goose so it, too, began to follow.	Children do the cat pose and MEOW like a cat.
Now there were four of them walking to the palace to meet the princess. There was the boy, the goose, the dog, and the cat. Soon the four met a turtle. The turtle liked the funny goose and its friends. The turtle, too, began to follow the parade of friends.	Children do the turtle pose and turtle hands.
Now they were five going to the palace to meet the princess. There was the boy, the goose, the dog, the cat, and the turtle. Soon they met another animal.	Children suggest animals to meet. Each time they do the animal poses, sounds, and behaviors. Every animal they meet wants to follow the boy and funny goose to see the princess. All children again make a single file parade and express the animal of their choice.
The boy, funny goose and all the many animals looked like an odd circus parade walking along toward the palace. Some of the animals were big. Some were small. Tell them, they look very funny following the goose.	

Storyline	Yoga Movement
When the boy, the goose, and the many animals (name them) reached the castle. The princess saw the boy, funny goose, and all the animals who looked like a big, funny circus parade with all the ways they walked and different noises they made. She began to smile.	Children make a small laugh, "Hee, hee, hee."
	Then, they pretend to make a huge belly laugh.
The princess gave out a teeny-weeny laugh. Soon the princess was laughing and laughing.	Finally, they do 'laughing yoga' by laughing like the princess non-stop for a long while. They can laugh on their backs while wiggling their arms and legs. This is Happy baby pose.
Even the King could hear the princess! He was very happy that his daughter finally was laughing.	Ask the children to hold hands and make a big circle. Invite them to step inwards while holding hands and make a little circle.
After the princess did such a long and big laugh, she changed. Now she could easily laugh.	Then step backwards and make a big circle. Do this a couple of times. Let children get silly and laugh.
The king gave the boy a bag of gold. And for all the animals the king made the grandest feast for them to eat.	Tell them they are all as silly and funny as the silly, funny goose.

Meditative Moment and Relaxation

Invite the children to close their eyes. Remember how when you laugh your body feels happy all over. Remember these happy feelings in your tippy toes and legs. Feel the happy feelings in your belly and in your heart. Make a big smile and feel the happy feeling inside everywhere, all over.

"Give yourselves a big hug and rub your head, face, chest, arms, legs, and feet." Have them lie down and do balloon breath. "Please close your eyes and relax."

While they relax, let it be silent, do guided imagery, or play music. At the end, children sit up and say, "You were awesome in Yoga Play."

Yoga Drama ~ The Monster Who Stole Red

Storyline	Yoga Movement
Once upon a time, there was a monster who stole red. He had a hairy body, huge feet, big ears, large teeth, a long-pointed nose, and long ears. He was not happy and so he did not want others to be happy.	Children walk like a monster with heavy feet thudding into floor, frowning faces. Perhaps growling.
This Monster wanted to make others sad, so he stole the color red.	Have red objects strewn around. Have one or a couple of children pretend to be the monster and pick up the red objects. They put the red things in a bag.
He took red from the stop light. He took red from the crayons. Red from the flowers. Red from the apples. Red from Santa's clothes and red from Valentines' day hearts. The monster steals red items and puts them in bag.	The other children say, "Oh no," every time something red is taken. They pretend to cry, making weeping sounds.
The children wanted to get the red back. So, they went to cat and asked, "How can we stop the Monster and get back all the red that was stolen." Cat said, "Do cat pose like me and you will be speedier." Then they say, "I think we should ask tree."	Children do cat pose. The children crawly speedily around.
The children asked tree, "How do we get red back?" The tree said, "I will give you the gift of strength. It will help you win over the monster." The tree gives each of them a stick and says, "This is so you remember you have strength."	Children take giant steps to find the tree. They do tree pose. Sticks are given to each child.
Then the children go to lion for help. They asked lion, "How do we get red back." Lion said, "I will give you courage." Lion gives each child a paper heart and said, "This is so you remember you have courage."	Children do lion pose and roar. A heart is given to each child.

Storyline	Yoga Movement
The children went to wise snake, "How do we get red back?" The snake said, "I will teach you to be wiser. You should do cobra pose and hiss like I do. I am giving you a smooth pebble to remember your wisdom.	The children do snake pose and hiss like the snake. A smooth stone is given to each child.
The children visited many animals to learn how to defeat the Monster and get back the red.	The children suggest which animals to ask. Then they do their poses and sounds. Each animal gives some attribute to the children. Each gives a simple gift.
The last animal the children ask was wise owl. Wise owl said, "Sit and close your eyes. Whisper softly these magic words, 'Baba nam kevalam, love is all there is. Then you can get the red from the Monster."	Children do the bird pose. They sit with their wings close to their sides and turn their heads as far as they can from side to side. Then the children sit and close their eyes and softly say, "Baba nam kevalam, love is all there is." (Whisper so softly only they can hear it and no one else.)
Now the children were ready to go to the Monster. They have all the abilities the animals had taught – strength, courage, bravery and the magic words. The children walked to where the Monster stayed.	Children puff out their chests and hold arms overhead in Warrior pose. Then they take giant steps towards the Monster without fear.
They saw that the Monster held the big bag in its arms. The bag was full of the red that it had taken. The children were not afraid. The children said, "Please, give us back our red." The Monster roared, "I will NOT!"	Children do the Warrior pose as they talk to the monster. They have the look of firm determination.
They remembered all the gifts that the animals had given to them. They began to sing, "Baba nam kevalam, love is all there is."	Children make the Namaste/Namaskar Warrior pose with palms together by their hearts.
"Stop," said the Monster, "You are making me nicer." The children did not stop singing. "Baba nam kevalam, love is all there is," they repeated.	Children sit and do the Namaste/Namaskar hand pose by their hearts and sing "Baba nam kevalam."

Storyline	Yoga Movement
Then the Monster opened the bag and the red flew out of the bag and went back to the stop light, to the flowers, to the apples, to the crayons and to all the red things' places.	Children are still sitting with Namaste/Namaskar gesture by their hearts with closed eyes, saying Baba nam kevalam.
"I feel all warm and fuzzy inside. I feel like doing good things. I feel like being a good friend. You have softened my heart."	The children hugged the Monster and it hugged the children. The Monster had become mean because it had no friends. The children had softened its heart by being friendly.
The monster and the children do the Namaste/Namaskar.	All do Namaste/Namaskar.

Meditative Moment and Relaxation

Invite the children, to sit and close their eyes. Take a restful breath in and out. Picture the color red. Red for Santa's suit and red for Valentine hearts. Then ask the children to lie on their backs and close their eyes and relax." While they relax, their Inner Friend is giving them a silent Namaste/Namaskar.

After a restful pause let the children wiggle, stretch and sit up. "You were awesome in yoga play. They do Namaste/Namaskar.

Yoga Drama ~ Wheels on the Bus Story

Storyline	Yoga Movement
Once upon a time the children wanted to go on a bus ride and see many places. So, they got on a school bus and sang while it drove them to new towns.	Children are in a line, facing the back of the child in front, hands on the shoulders in front. Walking together in a snake-like line.
Children sing: The wheels on the bus go, round and round. Round and round, round and round. The wheels on the bus go, round and round. So early in the morning.	Children sing the song and act it out.
The bus took them to _____ (name a local town.) In _____ they came upon Gray Rabbit.	Children do rabbit pose, wiggle their noses, and sniff.
Rabbit suggested to the children that they should go next to (name a local town.) So, the children got back on the bus and sang the bus song again until the bus arrived in _____ (name a local town.) There the children met Yellow Cat.	Children sing the bus song above while doing bus yoga. Then they did the cat pose and make cat sounds.
Cat told to the children that next they should visit _____ (name a local town) and meet Green Horse who lives there. So, the children got back on the bus and sang the bus song while it drove to the next town. In this manner the children visited various places and met many colored animals along the way. Each time they rode the bus singing the bus song.	Children sing the bus song. Then they do the horse pose which is like a dog pose and neigh. They can rear their front legs. Let children suggest places and animals to meet. They do their animal poses.
Finally, the sun was setting and the children had to go home. The bus drove straight back and dropped the children at their homes where they each went to sleep.	Children lie down in their 'homes' to go to sleep in the manner of their favorite animal that they visited today.

Meditative Moment and Relaxation

Children sit and close their eyes. They picture one animal they met today. It is a friend to them. The children give themselves a big hug and rub their heads, face, chest, arms, legs, and feet. Lie down and do balloon breath. Then ask the children to re-close their eyes and relax. When the children finish and sit up, tell them how awesome they were in yoga play.

Yoga Drama - Paloma and its Feathers

Storyline	Yoga Movement
Once upon a time, there was a most beautiful bird named Paloma. Its feathers were all colors of the rainbow. There was violet, indigo, blue, green, red, orange, and yellow-colored feathers. There were pink, brown, black, and gray feathers.	Ask the children their favorite color. Tell them Paloma may have that feather color for them. Children do bird pose.
Paloma liked the different creatures where she lived. The animals liked Paloma. One day the beautiful bird flew to a tall tree to look out around her.	The children fly around the room in a circle. Eventually they all do the tree pose.
Paloma sat in the tree looking around. She saw a baby rooster crying. Paloma flew to the rooster and asked, "Why are you crying?" The rooster told Paloma that it has lost a big feather in its tail.	Let the children do the rooster pose and crow like roosters.
Paloma felt sorry for the rooster. She pulled an orange feather from her own tail and gave it to the sad rooster. "Thank you," said rooster.	Let the children do grasshopper pose. One child is given an orange paper feather and improvises a feather dance.
Next Paloma met a grasshopper. The grasshopper began to cry. Paloma said, "Why are you crying?" "I am very cold," the grasshopper said. Paloma felt sorry for the grasshopper and gave it a green feather from its wing. The grasshopper wrapped the feather around its body and felt warmer. The grasshopper was very happy.	Children do cobra pose for grasshopper. One child is given a green paper feather and creates a feather dance.
The grasshopper told Paloma that in the bushes was a sad snake. "Maybe you can help the snake, too" it said. The snake said, "I am very cold." Again, Paloma felt sorry for the snake and gave it one of her own feathers to keep warm.	Children do cobra pose. One child is given a yellow paper feather and does a feather dance.

Storyline	Yoga Movement
Paloma saw a swallow nearby who looked sad so Paloma flew to the swallow.	Children do another variation of bird pose.
When Paloma reached the swallow, she asked, "Why are you so sad?" The swallow said, "I wish I had a colorful feather like you." Paloma gave the swallow one of her bright, red feathers. "Thank you," said the swallow and stuck the red flower in her tail.	One child receives a red paper feather and does a feather dance.
Paloma met more animals who also wished for one of her feathers. Each time Paloma gave them one.	Children suggest what animal poses they do. Each time Paloma gives away a feather. Each child is given a colored paper feather and does a feather dance.
Soon Paloma had fewer and fewer feathers. That night Paloma went to sleep and was cold from the loss of so many feathers. While she slept, a fairy came and saw Paloma with so few feathers on her body, cold and shivering in the night. The fairy touched Paloma with its magic wand.	All children are curled up on the floor, pretending to sleep. One child flies around the room with a stick wand and gently touches each child.
When Paloma awoke, her body was full of feathers again. But they were no longer the colors of the rainbow. Every feather was as white as fresh snow. This was the fairy's gift for being so kind to others. Paloma was happy with the white feathers and flew off into the sky.	All children awake with surprised expressions on their faces. All children receive white feathers. They do a feather dance and fly carefully around the room in a big circle.

Meditative Moment and Relaxation

Invite children to sit and close their eyes. Take a feather and touch each child's cheek gently. "Imagine that your body is very light. Your legs, arms, and heads are as light as feathers. You are feeling so light that you can easily float up into the sky like a cloud."

After a long pause, "Give yourselves a big hug. Please rub your head, face, chest, arms, legs, and feet. When you are finished, let's lie down and do balloon breath. Close your eyes and relax."

While they relax, let it be silent or play music. When the children sit up, tell the children how awesome they were in yoga play.

Yoga Drama ~ The Costume/Halloween Party

Storyline	Yoga Movement
Once upon a time the children wanted to have a Halloween (or a costume) Party. Everyone had to come to the party as a different animal.	
Ask each child, one by one, "What animal do you want to be?"	Children do the postures of their suggested animals. They make their sounds and movements.
There were many animals at the party. They decided to have a group hug. This is our circle hug. We are going to make a big hug and we are going to make a little hug.	Make a standing group hug. Let the children put their arms on each other shoulders in a big circle. Make a little hug by taking baby steps in towards the center until children's shoulders are touching. Change to holding hands in a big circle by walking back and stretching the arms. Then slowly, very slowly, children do baby steps in until they make a little circle. Repeat.
All the animals were stomping around the room.	Act out stomping animals in the circle.
All the animals were flying around the room.	Children do flying yoga. They fly around the room.
All the animals were twirling around the room.	Children do twirling yoga, twirling around the room.
All the animals went to sleep.	Children do sleeping yoga. All lie down and pretend to sleep.

Meditative Moment and Relaxation

Invite the children to sit so that they are not touching their neighbor and space is around them. Children close their eyes. "Feel space swirling all around you."

"Imagine your arms are getting bigger and bigger. Your arms are so big you can give a ginormous hug to all your friends, your neighbors, and your families. You are sending out a big hug to the world."

"Give yourselves a big hug. Rub your head, face, chest, arms, legs, and feet. When you are finished, let's lie down and do balloon breath. "Please close their eyes and relax."

While they relax, let it be silent or play music. After a long pause, ask the children to wiggle and stretch. "You were awesome in yoga play. Let's end with a Namaste/Namaskar. Thank you."

Yoga Drama~ Santa Needs Help

Storyline	Yoga Movement
Once upon a time, Santa was walking in the forest and his big, black boot got stuck in the mud. He pulled and pulled but could not get his boot free from the mud. Along came a dog and Santa said, "Excuse me, can you pull me from this mud puddle?" The dog tried to pull out Santa by using its mouth to pull Santa. It could not free Santa.	Children can walk around like Santa, pooching their bellies out. Putting their hands on their bellies, "Ho, ho, ho." Let children do the dog pose, pant like a dog, bark, and growl and do dog behaviors.
Soon a deer came by. Santa said, "Excuse me, can you pull me from this mud puddle?" Santa held the deer's horn and the deer tried to pull Santa out of the mud but it could not.	The children do deer pose.
Then a snake came by. Santa said, "Excuse me, can you pull me from this mud puddle?" Santa held the snakes' tail. The snake began to crawl and slither away to pull Santa out of the mud. But it could not do it.	The children do snake/cobra pose. They can hiss like a snake and do other snake behaviors, sticking out their tongues like snakes.
Children suggest others. Each time Santa says, "Can you pull me from this mud puddle?" But it cannot.	Suggest other animals. The children do their poses, behaviors, and sounds.
The animals said, "Let us all try to pull together!" Each animal took hold of a long rope and pulled.	Each child pretends they are an animal. Let them do its pose.
They said, "One, two, three, pull." Together their pull was so strong that Santa became free.	Then the adult holds an end of a rope like Santa did and the children hold the other end. The children pull the adult.
Santa said, "Thank you for helping" to each child, and shook each child's hand.	All take turns shaking the designated Santa's hand.

Meditative Moment and Relaxation

Invite the children to sit. They can cup their hands, one on top of the other, in their laps. "Please close your eyes. Santa will put a special gift for you in your hand. He will put it in your hands when your eyes are closed. Santa's gift can only be seen with closed eyes. His gift is love and looks like magical light. It is a very special gift. Children try to picture the Santa's light.

"Give yourselves a big hug. Rub your head, face, chest, arms, legs, and feet."

Children lie down and do balloon breath. Ask the children to close their eyes and relax. While they relax, let it there be silence or play music. After a long pause, the children may wiggle and stretch. Tell the children they were awesome in yoga play. Namaste./Namaskar.

Yoga Drama ~ The Lost Reindeer

Storyline	Yoga Movement
Once upon a time, before Christmas, one of Santa's reindeer, Comet, ran off to play with other deer in Evergreen Forest (name a forest near the children). Comet was having so much fun romping with the other deer it forgot about helping Santa.	Children do the deer pose. They romp and prance in circles with a partner.
Later, Santa checked on his reindeer to help them get ready for Christmas. He called, "Come Dasher, Dancer, Prancer, and Vixen. Come Comet, Cupid, Donner and Blitzen. Come Rudolph." All the deer ran to Santa, but not Comet. "Where is Comet?" asked Santa. The deer did not know. Santa called his elves and asked, "Where is Comet?" The elves did not know.	All the reindeer romp in one giant circle. Children walk on their knees pantomiming a small elf person.
Santa said to the elves, "All reindeer are here except Comet. You have to help me find Comet." So, the elves become like warriors on the quest to find the missing Comet. They walk into the mighty forest.	Children do warrior pose and take Warrior strides. Children do the tree pose, holding hands to be a forest.
They met a frog in the forest. The elves asked the frog, "Did you see Comet, Santa's reindeer?" The frog said, "No I it did not see Comet. You should ask the sparrow."	Children do frog pose.
They asked sparrow, "Did you see Comet, Santa's reindeer?" Sparrow said, "No, I did not see Comet. You should ask the turtle."	Children do sparrow pose. They tweet like a bird and flap their arms like wings.
The elves asked turtle, "Did you see Comet, Santa's reindeer?" Turtle said, "No, I did not see Comet. You should ask the ___." (Children suggest an animal.) Each animal says, "I did not see Comet the reindeer. You should ask _____."	They do the turtle pose and turtle hands. Children suggest the animals do their poses, and sounds. In this manner they do various poses

106

Storyline	Yoga Movement
The last animal says, "Yes, Comet is playing on top of the hill with all the forest deer." The elves hurried up the hill.	The children panto-mime walking up a hill with big steps and pant-ing effort.
At the top of the hill, there was Comet, playing with all the forest deer, romping and prancing.	Deer are romping and prancing. Children do Deer pose. Then they romp and prance.
The elves told Comet, "Please run home to Santa. Santa needs you." So, Comet ran as fast as he could back home to Santa.	Children may run in place.
When the elves got back to the workshop, Santa said, "Oh, thank you. I could not find him by myself." Santa gave each a hug. Then Santa gave each elf a special gift. Santa said, "I need all elves to sit very still and close your eyes. Now look inside your heads and find your favorite color."	Invite all to sit and close their eyes. In their heads picture a color. The color is a gift from Santa.
"This color is a special Christmas gift from Santa to you. The color is a tiny piece of happiness. But if you check on it over time. The color will grow and you will have even more happiness."	

Meditative Moment and Relaxation

Invite all to sit and close their eyes and picture again their favorite color, they are trying to make it grow. When finished, they are asked to give themselves a big smile. Then give themselves a big hug like Santa hugged his elves.

Children rub their head, face, chest, arms, legs, and feet. They lie down and do balloon breath. Then ask the children to close their eyes and relax. Teacher sings, "Baba nam kevalam. Love is all there is." While they relax, let there be silence.

After a long pause, ask the children to stir and stretch. "You were awesome in yoga play. Namaste/ Namaskar."

Yoga Drama ~ The Elephant's Big Nose

Storyline	Yoga Movement
Once upon a time, there was a baby elephant named Jumbo. She had a giant, long nose, which was even big for an elephant's nose. That was why the animals called her Jumbo.	Ask the children to make elephant noses with their arms. Raise their trunk/noses and trumpet like an elephant.
Jumbo was a happy elephant who liked to help other animals. One day a cat was stuck in a tree. Jumbo wanted to help the cat. Jumbo stood under the tree and raised her big nose, picked the cat up and brought it to the ground. The cat was happy to get down.	Children do a cat pose and meow like a cat. Be a happy cat. Some children can do tree pose.
Jumbo heard a dog barking and went to it. The dog said, "I am lost and cannot smell where my Mama is. Can you smell her with your big nose?" Jumbo smelled the air and said, "Your Mama is that way." The dog was happy and ran off that way.	Children do dog pose and bark like a dog. Let them move their hips like a dog wagging its tail. Then sniff like a dog does. Be a happy dog.
After a while, Jumbo saw a sad deer. This deer was sad because it could not reach some leaves on a tree that it wanted to eat. Jumbo pulled a branch down for the deer to eat.	The children do deer pose. Be a happy deer.
Next Jumbo saw a rabbit trying to reach a turnip in a hole, but it could not reach the turnip with its small paws. Jumbo stuck its big nose into the hole and pulled out the turnip for rabbit.	Children do rabbit pose. They sniff like rabbits. They can hop like rabbits. Be a happy rabbit.
Jumbo saw a small sparrow had fallen out of its nest. With its big nose, Jumbo lifted the sparrow back to its nest.	Children make the bird/sparrow pose.

Storyline	Yoga Movement
A snake wanted to cross a creek, but it could not swim. Jumbo picked up the snake and put it on the other side of the creek.	Children do the cobra pose.
A tiny green grasshopper wanted to cross the creek, too. Jumbo let the grasshopper hop on its nose and she swam across the creek to the other side. Grasshopper hopped off.	Children do grasshopper pose. They jump around like grasshoppers.
A hunter came by looking for his arrow. The hunter found it stuck in a tree. As he was a good hunter who did not hurt animals, the elephant pulled out the arrow and gave it to him. Jumbo helped many creatures with its long, strong nose.	Children do bow and arrow pose. They can do the warrior pose. Ask the children to suggest other animals that need help by Jumbo's nose and do their poses.
Jumbo was happy to help others. Jumbo closed its eyes and his heart felt full of love from helping so many animals.	Children can sit and share what they did the last time they helped someone. How did they feel after helping?

Meditative Moment and Relaxation

Invite the children to sit and with their eyes closed. After they close their eyes, ask them to touch one finger to their nose. "Feel how small your nose is. It is not big like Jumbo's. But you have a big heart. It is full of love." Children open their eyes Ask, "Make a heart shape with both of your hands and blow it away, sending love to your parents. Make more hearts and send them to your friends, and to anyone you want."

Ask the children to give themselves a big hug. They massage their head, face, chest, arms, legs, and feet. Children lie down and do balloon breath. Then, they close their eyes and relax. After a long pause, ask the children to wiggle and stretch. Tell the children they were awesome in yoga play.

Yoga Drama ~ Row Row Your Boat Time

Storyline	Yoga Movement
Once upon a time, the children wanted to take a boat ride and visit Strange Island. They got into a big, row boat and began to row while singing: "Row, row, row your boat. Gently down the stream. Merrily, merrily, merrily, merrily. Life is but a dream."	Children can sit and hold each other's hands in one big circle. They move their arms together like they are rowing while they sing.
The children reached Strange Island. They walked down the island path. On the island they saw a barking cat and greeted it. They remarked, "Isn't that strange that the cat is barking like a dog?"	The children walk in a circle, as they go down an island path. Then children do cat pose and bark. How weird!
The children walked down the island path. Next the children met a meowing dog and greeted it. They said, "Isn't that odd to meet a meowing dog?"	The children walk in a circle, as they go down an island path. They do dog pose and meow like a cat.
The children walked down the island path and saw other strange things. There were tall palm trees with apples growing on them and apple trees with bananas growing.	They again walk in a circle, going further on the island path. Children do a tree pose and then do somersault rolls like apples. They do tree pose and pencil roll like bananas.
Children meet many more creatures.	Children suggest other strange animals and do their poses. (T Rex making mouse sounds, birds making monkey sounds, ants making lion sounds.)
The sun was going down. It was time to return home so the children went back to their big row boat and began to row towards home. The sky was blue and the water was calm. The children sang and rowed until they reached home.	Children make a circle and hold hands. Then they sing the Row Row Row Your Boat, very fast and move their arms fast. Then they sing slowly and move their arms slowly.

Storyline	Yoga Movement
In the distance, they heard the roar of lightning and they thought they heard the sounds of birds flying, making silly monkey sounds. What a strange place!	Children do lightning pose and do bird pose with monkey chatters.

Meditative Moment and Relaxation

"Please sit 'legs crossed applesauce' and fold your hands in your laps. Close your eyes and make pictures in your head that you are on a rowboat in water, floating on a calm lake. You can hear the waves lapping on the shore. The sky is blue, and the sun is shining warm sunbeams on your skin."

After a short while, invite the children to open their eyes and give themselves a big hug for doing such a good job rowing the boat. Then they rub their head, face, chest, arms, legs, and feet. Afterwards, the children lie down, close the eyes, do balloon breath, and rest.

When the children sit up, tell them that they were awesome in yoga play and Namaste/Namaskar each other.

Yoga Drama - Fluffy Kitten Can't Sleep

Storyline	Yoga Movement
Once upon a time there was a fluffy, soft kitten. Mama Cat would lick the fluffy kitten and take care of her with much gentleness.	Children do cat pose. Give the children items such as soft cotton balls, fur, and other things. They practice gentle touching.
When it was time to sleep, Mama Cat sang a special song to the fluffy kitty to help it fall quickly asleep. She sang: Soft kitty, warm kitty, little ball of fur. Happy kitty, sleepy kitty, purr, purr, purr.	Children curl up into a pose in which kitties sleep.
One day Mama Cat went hunting and left her baby kitten with her dog friend to watch over her. After frolicking, Fluffy Kitten wanted to sleep and asked dog, "Can you please sing my lullaby." But dog said, "I do not know your lullaby." Dog sadly whimpered and whined regretably. Fluffy Kitten cried unhappily, "Mew, Mew."	Children do dog pose. Children are like Dog and sadly whimper, whine, and shake their head no. They do cat pose and mew pathetically with sadness.
Finally, dog said, "Let's go ask snake." They went to snake. Fluffy Kitten asked, "Can you please sing my lullaby?" But snake said, "I do not know your lullaby and hisses sadly. Go ask bird."	Children do snake pose. They stick out their tongues. They hiss like snakes. They act like Fluffy Kitten and mew sadly.
They went to bird, and Fluffy Kitten asked, "Can you please sing my lullaby?" But bird said, "I do not know your lullaby and peeps sadly." Dog and Fluffy Kitten asked other animals, "Can you sing my lullaby?" But all the animals say, "I do not know your lullaby. Ask _____."	Children do the bird pose and make a bird with their hands. Bird peeps sadly. Have the children suggest other animals. The children do their poses and express sadness.
Finally, dog says, "Let's go back home and wait for Mama Cat."	All animals walk home in a circle.

Storyline	Yoga Movement
When they got home Mama Cat was already there. She gave Fluffy Kitten a big hug. Then she sang her lullaby to help Fluffy Kitten go to sleep: Soft kitty, warm kitty, little ball of fur. Happy kitty, sleepy kitty, purr, purr, purr. And Fluffy Kitten slept soundly.	All children hug and curl up when they hear the Lullaby. They make sleeping kitty sounds.

Meditative Moment and Relaxation

"Please cup your hands. Imagine that you have a small fluffy kitten in your hands." Put a cotton ball or something soft in each hand. "Close your eyes and try to hear it purring for you."

Children give themselves hugs like from their mothers. They rub their head, face, chest, arms, legs, and feet. Then they lie down, close their eyes, and do balloon breath. Tell the children to imagine they are lying on a soft fluffy bed. Ask the children:

- Lift your (right) leg. Put it down. Breathe in and breathe out.
- Lift your (other or left) leg. Put it down, and rest it. Breathe in and breathe out.
- Lift your right arm. Put it down, and rest it. Breathe in and breathe out.
- Lift your (other or left) arm. Put it down. Breathe in and breathe out.
- Lift your head. Put it down, and rest it. Breathe in and breathe out.
- Relax your legs and feet. Breathe in and breathe out.
- Relax your arms and hands. Breathe in and breathe out.
- Relax your chest. Breathe in and breathe out.
- Relax your back. Breathe in and breathe out.
- Relax your neck and head. Breathe in and breathe out.
- Relax your whole body. Breathe in and breathe out.

Then, after a suitable pause of a minute or two, ask the children to wiggle and stretch. Tell the children, "You were awesome in yoga play. Namaste/Namaskar."

Footnotes

[1]http://www.rabbishefagold.com/about/, accessed June 12, 2017.
[2]Kabir, translated by Robert Bly, "The Simple Purification," *News of the Universe: Poems of Twofold Consciousness*, Counterpoint Press, 2015.

References

Circle of Love, Editor Av. Anandamitra Ac., Ananda Marga Board of Education, Manila, Philippines 1980. (Illustrations by Av. Anandarama Ac. And Didi Rainjita Brcii.)

About the authors

MJ "MahaJyoti" Glassman lives in Denver Colorado. She has spent thirty years working in a yoga-based preschool. MJ teaches multi-generational adults and facilitates yoga teacher training in the USA and around the world. An avid meditator, yoga enthusiast, and social service advocate, she participates in community projects that ease the suffering of other members of her community.

Nancy "Niiti" Gannon has twenty-five years of experience in early childhood education and children's yoga. Besides teaching children, she is an avid meditator and a registered yoga teacher. Other publications by Nancy are *Teach Me to Fly*, an early childhood education publication, and *Meetings with my Master*, an autobiographical experience with her Yoga Master.

www.ingramcontent.com/pod-product-compliance
Lightning Source LLC
Chambersburg PA
CBHW081000120626
46546CB00010B/2976